Reaching and Keeping Tweenagers

Dr Peter Brierley

This survey was sponsored by:

Baptist Union of Great Britain
Boys' Brigade
Church Army
Church Pastoral Aid Society
Crusaders
Evangelical Alliance
J W Laing Trust
Salesians of Don Bosco
Spring Harvest
Youth for Christ

*All royalties from this book will go towards
the cost of further research for the Church.*

 **Christian Research**

November 2002

The right of Peter Brierley to be identified as the author of this work has been asserted by him in accordance with the Copyright, Designs and Patents Act 1988

First British edition November 2002

ISBN 1 85321 147 8

A Workbook has been produced in association with this volume
and should be used with it wherever possible (ISBN 1 85321 150 8).

Published by
Christian Research
Vision Building,
4 Footscray Road,, Eltham,, London SE9 2TZ
Phone: 020 8294 1989   Fax: 020 8294 0014
Email: admin@Christian-research.org.uk
Web: www.christian-research.org.uk
and: www.ukchristianhandbook.org.uk

British Library Cataloguing Data
A catalogue record for this book is available from the British Library.

Designed and produced for the publisher by:
Paul Jones Associates, 98 Eden Way, Beckenham, Kent BR3 3DH

Printed by:
Cox & Wyman, England

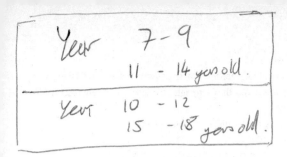

Year 7 - 9
11 - 14 yers old.

Year 10 - 12
15 - 18 yers old.

To my special colleagues Heather Wraight,
who facilitated the Focus Groups,
Gwen Gowers, Kim Miles and Vicky Wharton,
without whom this study would simply never
have been carried out and who helped shoulder
the burden in the heat of the day.

Also to my granddaughter Ashleigh,
who in two years time will become a Tweenager,
and has made me additionally conscious
that this is not an academic exercise
but something crucial for the Kingdom.

Also to Sue Plater, John Flack, Nick Margesson,
Chris Radley, Brian Pearson and Mike Smith,
the Board members at the time who urged
this study forwards.

Contents

Introduction

It was real scary as the analysis began. I came into work one morning and my colleagues said to me, "What's up?" "I've been trying
to understand the figures from this 1998 English Church Attendance
Survey," I replied. "I've been looking at the number of children
under 15 in the church. They've dropped nearly half a million in the
last nine years. We're losing kids at the rate of 1,000 a week! Two
churches in five in England have no children's or youth work at all."

"What can we do?" they asked.

"We've got to find out why." We all agreed. So did others serving with youth organisations and battling it out at the front line.
Crusaders, Youth For Christ, the Salesians of Don Bosco, Church
Pastoral Aid Society, the Baptist Union of Great Britain, Spring
Harvest, J W Laing Trust and the Evangelical Alliance were all concerned and responded to letters asking for help with a major new
study specially aimed at youth. Others also supported the study in
different ways, like Boys' Brigade and Church Army. In addition a
much wider body of people kindly agreed to act on the Council of
Reference.[1]

A small planning committee under the chairmanship of
Richard Bromley, Director of Local Ministry, Youth for Christ,
began to consider what should be investigated and how. The project
was called Reaching And Keeping Early Secondaries (RAKES).
The outcome was that four groups of young people were identified:

- Those who were currently still in church
- Those who had been in church but had left
- Those who had never gone regularly to church
- Those who attended Christian events or youth clubs but who
  didn't go to church regularly.

It was agreed that the main focus of the study should be young people aged 10 to 14 (school years 6 to 10), though inevitably some 9 and 15 year olds were caught up in the sweep. We approached schools, churches, and parachurch agencies asking for young people to complete a questionnaire, and also held two Focus Groups, one among churchgoing young people and one among non-churchgoers. It was perhaps especially appropriate that this survey took place in 2001, the UNICEF "Year of the Child". State and Church (Anglican and Catholic) Schools were approached.

There has been a huge amount of support for this study, and virtually everyone we approached has seen its importance and supported it as far as they could. We are tremendously thankful for this interest and concern, and grateful to all who have helped in whatever way.

But of course, it's what all these young people said that's really important – so read on!

---

[1]A full list of sponsors appears on the title page. A complete list of the Council of Reference is given in Appendix 1.

Hi, Tweens!

Most British children move from junior school to secondary school around the age of 11. Some go to a middle school, but these are being phased out, and some 7% go to public school at 13, but for the large majority, the change comes the year they celebrate their 11th birthday.

Teenage attitudes and values develop gradually over several years, starting in the final phase of junior school. Hence the focus of this study on these "early and pre-teens" as the survey questionnaire was headed, or "early secondaries" as it was otherwise described. A more convenient word for this age-group is "Tweenagers", a term originally coined by marketing professionals, so that's what we'll call them.

Why the concern?

The English Church Attendance Survey and earlier English Church Censuses have shown that the total number of children under 15 attending church (of all denominations) on a Sunday was:
- 1,400,000 in 1979,
- 1,200,000 in 1989, and
- 720,000 in 1998.

The 200,000 decrease in the 1980s more than doubled in the 1990s. The 1990s decrease averaged 1,000 children a week leaving church, equivalent to 50,000 a year, or half a million, 500,000, in a decade. The rate of decline is not strictly linear, but even so it has been suggested that if these trends continue, by 2016 the number of children under 15 in English churches could be as low as 225,000.[1]

Much concern has been expressed at the huge decline: the Church Pastoral Aid Society [CPAS], for example, aims to mount a major attempt to give every child in the country an "opportunity to make their own choice about the Christian faith"[2]. A leaflet is available about their campaign entitled "A heart for children"[3].

"The church must stop the haemorrhage of its young people and banish the generation gap from God's Kingdom," writes teacher and author of Sunday school materials Mrs Geraldine Witcher, and gives a whole book to explain how[4].

Isn't the decline just normal population change?

In fact, quite the contrary! There were 9,150,000 children under 15 in England in 1991, and 9,440,000 in 2001, an increase of nearly 300,000; the number is projected to decline 600,000 to 8,830,000 children by 2011, a decrease of 6%. The decline is not necessarily the same among churchgoing and non-churchgoing families, but nevertheless a small proportion of the future decline may be for natural reasons rather than anything to do with the church as such.

Who gave information?

The upper third (10–14 year olds) of this under 15 age-group was chosen for this study partly because of the educational and physical changes that occur in this five year period (which may influence their feelings towards the church), but also because it is during these years that many parents give their children freedom to choose whether or not they wish to continue coming with them to church.

A random selection of ministers was asked to distribute forms to the 10–14 age-group in their church or Sunday School[5]; 549 forms were returned from them. Just over 100 schools in the same towns as these churches were asked if they would allow one or more classes to complete the questionnaires, and more than a third agreed, returning in total 1,296 forms. In addition, forms were distributed to various Christian organisations working with young people of this age range and 327 forms were returned, giving a grand total of 2,172 forms. Thanks so much to all who helped in this exercise!

The returned forms were distributed across the different school years as shown below, where Year 6 is largely 10 year olds, Year 7 are aged 11 and so on up to Year 10 who are 14, and Year 11 who are 15.

Figure 1.1: Number of forms returned by school year

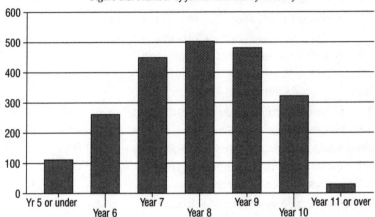

This is a very fair spectrum of the relevant target group. For convenience the few in Year 11 or over have been added to those in Year 10, and those in Year 5 or under to those in Year 6 for analysis. Nearly half, 47%, of the respondents were boys, a little under the population proportion of 51% for this age. The Focus Groups had a similar representation of ages, with the 7 girls and 10 boys who attended being 4 from Year 6, 4 from Year 7, 5 from Year 8, 3 from Year 9 and 1 from Year 10.

One question asked what grades they achieved for their school work. Their answers showed a range across the full spectrum, but more in the higher grades, indicating an ability to answer the questions sensibly (though whether they all did so is another matter!). Those aged 14 tended to get the lowest grades; full details are in Appendix 4, Table A4/1. Girls claimed higher grades than boys, as per Appendix 4, Table A4/2.

- 34% A grades
- 51% B
- 13% C
- 2% D, E or F.

Naturally we were also interested in whether they felt they were Christian or not. They replied as follows:

- 55% were Christian
- 24% were not sure if they were Christian
- 14% had never been a Christian
- 3% were no longer Christian, and
- 4% belonged to another religion, slightly less than in the general population.

However, being a Christian and regularly attending a place of worship is not the same thing! When asked if they now went, or had ever gone, to church or Sunday School, they replied:

- 36% went to church regularly
- 18% went to church occasionally
- 22% used to go, but didn't now
- 24% had never been.[6]

This is a very reasonable cross selection of the various kinds of experiences that were being explored. When the form mentioned "church" we asked the 4% who belonged to other religions to substitute "temple", "synagogue", "mosque", etc. The questionnaire did not include a question on ethnic origins.

Experience of church

The respondents' churchgoing varied by age, gender and academic success (as measured by the grades they usually obtained). Figure 1.2 illustrates how their churchgoing varied with their age.

The regular churchgoers decline with age, with the largest drop between those aged 11 and 12, when young people have been in secondary school for a year or so. Those who go to church only occasionally drop in number at the same time, although with a marginal increase later. The change is, however, even more noticeable among those who are no longer churchgoers, increasing between those aged 10 and 11, the year they move from junior to secondary school. It is this transition which is the key dividing line.

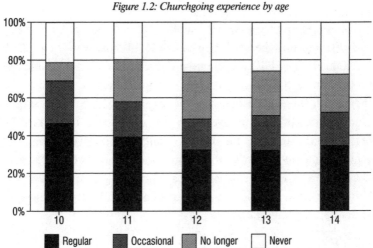

Figure 1.2: Churchgoing experience by age

All ten Tweenagers in the churchgoing Focus Group attended church regularly, though not necessarily every week. However, of the non-churchgoing group, one used to attend and all the others had been to church for a wedding, christening or on parade with a uniformed organisation. The one who used to attend was brought by a friend when she was in Year 7 and went 'on and off' for about 18 months.

Several researchers, perhaps especially in the UK Professor Leslie Francis, have explored the reasons why women tend to go to church more than men. The same was true of the boys and girls in this sample as Table 1.3 shows: more girls went regularly, more boys went occasionally or never. However, girls were the more likely to have dropped out.

Table 1.3: Church attendance by gender

Gender	Regular	Occasional	Lapsed	Never
	%	%	%	%
Boy	32	20	19	29
Girl	39	17	25	19
Overall	**36**	**18**	**22**	**24**

The grades young people usually obtained also varied between churchgoers and others[7]. Nearly half, 46%, of those who got grade A (or claimed they did!) were regular churchgoers, almost double the proportion of those who no longer or never went to church. Are those with most academic success (as measured by their school grade) more attracted or loyal to church, or does this but reflect the often-stated claim that the church is middle-class? Those who got the lowest grades (D, E or F) were more likely to be occasional churchgoers. The percentage of those normally getting Grades B or C increased the further they were from being regular churchgoers! Details are in Table 1.4.

Table 1.4: Church attendance by academic success

Usual Grade	Regular %	Occasional %	Lapsed %	Never %	Overall %
A	46	33	28	24	**34**
B	44	53	56	57	**51**
C	9	11	14	18	**13**
D, E, F	1	3	2	1	**2**

Who are these young people?

They may be called Tweenagers, but their generation has been given plenty of other names as well! Their parents were initially called the Buster Generation, as in a sense they broke (or "bust") the population boom in which their parents (that is, our sample's grandparents) had been born. In Britain this term was never very popular and for a while Tweenagers' parents were called the Thatcher Children, but this rapidly disappeared once Mrs Thatcher was no longer Prime Minister! Sometimes they were called the Millennium Generation, as the generation which would reach adulthood at the start of the new millennium, or "Beepers" as they grew up with the new IT technology. A much more exciting term quickly caught on in the early 1990s from a book by Douglas Coupland[8] – the X Generation or Generation X. Many other books and articles[9] have followed about this generation.

Their children somewhat naturally are called Generation Y, but they have also been called other names, of which "Mosaics" is the most common, since their worldview is made up of scattered pieces each with part of the total picture, like a Roman mosaic. Their children, Generation Z, may also be called the "Kaleidoscopes", since they are likely to make more than one picture (or worldview) with the pieces they put together. The full generational sequence is shown in Table 1.5.

Table 1.5: Six Generations of British People

Generation	Other names	Years of birth	Age range in 2002	Population size in 2002[10]
Seniors		1900–26	76+	4.1 million
Builders	Boosters, Maturity	1927–45	57 to 75	10.9 million
Boomers	Baby Boomers	1946–64	38 to 56	14.9 million
Busters	Generation X	1965–83	19 to 37	15.6 million
Mosaics	Generation Y	1984–02	0 to 18	14.3 million
Kaleidoscopes	Generation Z	2003–21	To be born!	0 million

While many comparisons have been made of Generation X and its forebears, few have compared Generations X, Y and Z. One of those who has, however, is the minister of Christ Church, Barnton, Northwich, Cheshire, who has kindly given permission for us to quote from his analysis in the following Tables.[11] We have slightly adapted his work and added the column for Generation Z.[12]

Tweenagers are the upper end of Generation Y, in between Generations X and Z. They are "children becoming teens 'at the age of 10'"[14]. Tables 1.6 – 1.10 help to position some of their attitudes and other characteristics.

Table 1.6: Family and social characteristics of Generations X, Y and Z

Gen X "Busters"	Gen Y "Mosaics"	Gen Z "Kaleidoscopes"
The Family		
• Dysfunctional/ broken homes	• Like Gen-X but more single parent families	• Even more single-parent families
• Latch-key generation; both parents working to boost family income and compete in consumer society	• Increasingly complex due to increasing divorce rate	• Families with "serial" fathers
	• Most want to marry, and have children	
Friendship		
• High value	• Conform to peers	• Mobile phones used to keep in constant contact
• The "aborted generation"; unwanted	• The designer label generation	
	• Image & acceptability	
Pastoral care		
• Perceived as normative and normal	• Same as Gen X?	• Same as Gen Y?
Gender roles		
• Prefer husband-wife team	• Increasing female assertion has left men confused as to their role	• Equality at home extends to the workplace
• Egalitarian marriage		
• Option of doing your own thing		
Leisure		
• Value leisure more than work or things; "hang out"	• Very brand-conscious	• Alcohol, drugs and smoking normative from an early age
	• Clubbing, alcopops, smoking, illegal drugs	
Media		
• Grew up with 4 TV channels and the beginning of satellite	• Growing up with multiple channels	• Multi-purpose computer-cum-TV; mobile video laptop

Table 1.7: Personal characteristics of Generations X, Y and Z

Gen X "Busters"	Gen Y "Mosaics"	Gen Z "Kaleidoscopes"
Thinking		
• Narrative, non-linear	• Just do it	• Internet-stimulated
Feelings		
• Vote their feelings; express emotion	• Pessimistic; raised in an "anaesthetic" age	• Return to Gen X?
Sexuality		
• Associated sex with self-destruction; AIDS	• Recreational sex	• Even fewer inhibitions
• Greater awareness of sexuality	• Few inhibitions	• Start earlier
		• More teenage pregnancies
Information		
• Computers	• Sophisticated computers and the internet	• More than one story emerges from identical facts
Conflict		
• Direct, open, honest	• Same as Gen X?	• Same as Gen Y?

Table 1.8: Values and beliefs of Generations X, Y and Z

Gen X "Busters"	Gen Y "Mosaics"	Gen Z "Kaleidoscopes"
Values		
• Ignore and ridicule	• Markedly tolerant towards drug-taking, homosexuality, sex & violence in films	• Greater concern for the poor and disadvantaged
• Microwave		
• Want everything yesterday		• Right and wrong determined without regard for good and evil
• "Politically correct"	• Morality is decided by consensus; things right or wrong if we say so	
• Embarrassed by absolutes; relativistic		
Christianity		
• No spiritual or biblical compass	• What's Christianity?	• Around 20% will be baptised, and 20% marry in church
• Form your own opinion		
Devotional life		
• Find discipline hard but long for spiritual things	• Same as Gen X?	• Spiritual longing outworked in unconventional ways

Table 1.9: Economic and working characteristics of Generations X, Y and Z

Gen X "Busters"	Gen Y "Mosaics"	Gen Z "Kaleidoscopes"
Economics		
• Disadvantaged • Burdened with Boomers' debts • Sense of hopelessness	• More confident • Want to own their own businesses • Independent	• Use internet for shopping and services
Work		
• See job primarily as a means to an end • "Have integrity" • Function best in teams • Many jobs in lifetime, often meaning displacement or travel • Work for the good life	• Desire to improve themselves • Explosion of management techniques • Rapid technological change and mergers fosters adaptability	• More home-workers • More shared jobs (because wanting more leisure)? • Technology will be tops
Expectations		
• Survival • Limited horizons • Simple solutions • Have given up the idea of changing the world • Are afraid and angry	• Want to own their own businesses • Want work in business and finance	• Same as Gen Y?
Stress		
• High levels of stress at home and at work • High peer group and personal expectations	• Very high stress	• Will use internet chat rooms to share emotional highs
Risk		
• Risk takers	• Very high risk takers	• Careful to avoid parents' mistakes
Commitment		
• Short-term • Self-fulfilment	• Same as Gen X?	• Same as Gen Y?
Leadership		
• Participatory, team, respects the genuine, authentic, open	• Same as Gen X?	• Same as Gen Y?

Table 1.10: State characteristics of Generations X, Y and Z

Gen X "Busters"	Gen Y "Mosaics"	Gen Z "Kaleidoscopes"
Institutions		
• Sceptical	• Even more sceptical • They expect less and less of government; an apolitical generation	• Even more apolitical than their parents
Attitude to authority		
• Little respect but exalt the community and seek personal relationships	• Older people are an embarrassing irrelevance, well past sell-by date! • More respect for doctors, police & teachers than company directors, considered little better than politicians & journalists	• Acceptance of euthanasia? • Declining respect for anyone except friends and peers

What types of Tweenagers are there?

Clearly all Tweenagers are not the same. George Barna, a researcher based in California, has wide experience of evaluating different groups of people. He suggests that Mosaics, Generation Y, fall into four types:[14]

1) Interactives[15]

They dominate. "These are young people who are highly personable and develop their lifestyle according to relational possibilities and parameters. Nearly half of the teenage population, this segment operates with a stream of consciousness approach to problem solving while remaining sensitive to the needs and feelings of those with whom they have contact."

2) Dynamos

"Represent about a quarter of the teen world. These are the aggres-

sive, focussed, driven individuals who are effective at problem-solv-
ing and are above-average producers. However, they also irritate
some with their relentless energy, competitiveness and self-
assurance."

3) Stabilisers
"Provide continuity and consistency wherever they are found.
Roughly one-fifth of the teen contingent, they are appreciated for
their loyalty, thoroughness and predictability. They are also criticised for their rigidity and lack of creativity."

4) Evaluators
"At fewer than 1 of out of 10 teens, these are detail-orientated individuals who are continually assessing situations and people, and
insist on accuracy and completeness. They place lofty demands upon
themselves – and others. Their perfectionist tendencies and aversion
to risk-taking can frustrate others."

In another part of the same book, George Barna explains why
this group should be called "mosaic":
• Their lifestyles are an eclectic combination of traditional and
  alternative activities
• They are the first generation among whom a majority exhibit a
  non-linear style of thinking – a mosaic, connect-the-dots-however-
  you-choose approach
• Their relationships are much more racially integrated and fluid
  than any we have seen [before]
• Their core values are the result of a cut-and-paste mosaic of feelings, facts, principles, experiences and lessons
• Their primary information and connection – the internet – is the
  most bizarre, inclusive and ever-changing pastiche of information
  ever relied upon by humankind
• The central spiritual tenets that provide substance to their faith are
  a customised blend of multiple-faith views and religious practices[16].

Tweenagers are important!

Scripture Union staff member Gethin Russell-Jones, speaking at a consultation they organised in March 2001, said, "A lot of churches put resources into older teenagers and young people, but Tweenagers are often ignored because they are in between. The blame lies in the fact that adults in the Church are so culturally distant from the culture of Tweenagers."[17] CPAS undertook a "Finding the Path" tour in the autumn of 2001 for leaders of Pathfinder groups[18] to give such training in Tweenager culture,[19] and have produced the Search Engine CD.[20] At the beginning of 2001 the Church of Scotland launched CHOK (Children o' the Kirk) as a new initiative for reaching 8 to 14 year olds.[21]

The Church of England had shown its concern earlier by setting up a Working Party on youth work in the Church of England under the chairmanship of the then Bishop of Carlisle, the Rt Rev Ian Harland. It was published for discussion at the July 1996 Synod under the title *Youth A Part*[22]. Gill Brentford, a member of the Working Party, indicated that they were driven by a common vision of a "Church where young people participate fully and actively at every level."[23] The Report illustrated this in part by stating that in 1994 there were as few as 102 young men and 108 young women aged 14–17 serving on Parochial Church Councils [PCCs] in England (out of a total of 205,952 PCC members, or 0.1%)[24]. In 2001 Margaret Withers was appointed for 5 years to act as the Archbishop's Officer for children's evangelism, with her focus "reaching those children who don't otherwise have any contact with the church"[25].

Such activity shows that churches and agencies recognise the crucial importance of the Tweenager age-group. In July 1997 a woman who had supposedly been sterilised gave birth and successfully sued her hospital consultant. She was awarded £113,000, of which £105,000 was deemed to be the cost of bringing up her child.[26] Such costs will presumably be incurred by Christian parents as well

as non-Christian. How much will it cost to help Tweenagers understand and respond to the message of the Christian gospel?

One of the churches replying to the 1998 English Church
Attendance Survey[27] said that out of a normal congregation of 135 –
twice the average Anglican church – it had only 12 young people
aged 11 to 15, and only 3 boys aged under 10. Many churches would
rejoice to have so many!

At a seminar in Southend in April 2000 a group of clergy voted
that the most important characteristic of those of Gen X age was
that they were "radical – let them loose!"[28] The same is true of
Generation Y and Tweenagers.

If present trends continue, the proportion of young people in
English churches will drop drastically:

- In 1979, 26% of England's 5.4 million churchgoers were
  under 15
- In 1989 it was 25% of 4.7 million
- In 1998 it was 19% of 3.7 million
- If these trends continue, by 2020 it will be 4% of 1.8 million.[29]

It is imperative that this doesn't happen! Let us work to make
the forecast false.

This Chapter shows ...

- There was a good response to the survey from young people aged
  10 to 14, with replies coming from across all sectors of interest.
- There was a very adequate mix by age, usual school grade, whether
  they called themselves Christian and their experience of church.
- While we are calling this age-group Tweenagers in this book, they
  are a sub-group of a generation often called "Mosaics".
- This is a critical age-group for the church since, if nothing changes,
  their numbers are likely to rapidly diminish in the years ahead.

NOTES

[1] *The Tide is Running Out,* Peter Brierley, Christian Research, 2000, Page 98.

[2] Article "New bid to reach children" in the *Church of England Newspaper,* 28 July 2000, Page 1. The work would be headed up by Mrs Penny Frank.

[3] Details of the CPAS Children's Evangelism Initiative are available from Miss Janet Arter, heart@cpas.org.uk, or Rev Philip Mounstephen for the results of his ECS affiliated group survey, or through their new website, launched June 2002 www.heartforchildren.com.

[4] *Youth in Exodus,* Geraldine Witcher, Highland Books, Godalming, Surrey, 2002.

[5] We have used the term "Sunday School" throughout this book, although aware that many churches call this activity Sunday Club or a variety of other, more imaginative, names.

[6] The correlation between this set of figures and the previous set is given in Table 2.4.

[7] This was also true in the Focus Groups, but with only two held the difference could also have been due to the different backgrounds of the young people in the groups.

[8] *Generation X, Tales from an accelerated culture,* D Coupland, St Martin's Press, USA, 1991.

[9] For example, *From Separation to Synergy, receiving the richness of Generation X,* Kath Donovan, Zadok Paper S106, Zadok Institute, Winter 2000; *Generation NeXt,* George Barna, Regal Books, Ventura, California, USA, 1995; *Generation X, Attitudes and Lifestyles, Survey Report,* Peter Brierley, Christian Research, March 2001; *Why do they do that – Understanding Teenagers,* Nick Pollard, Lion, 1998; *Boomers, Xers, and Other Strangers,* Dr Rick & Kathy Hicks, Tyndale, 1999; *Generation Y, young, gifted and self-centred,* article by Mark Henderson in The Times, 14/11/98.

[10] *Population Trends,* National Statistics, The Stationery Office, No 104, Summer 2001, Table 1.5.

[11] His full analysis includes assessing Builders and Boomers also, which is not given here. He may however be contacted on keith@barntonv1.freeserve.co.uk

[12] This is based on an article in *Quadrant,* September 2001, Christian Research.

[13] Article with this title by Rhys Williams in *The Independent,* 31 December 1998, page 5.

[14] *Real Teens,* George Barna, Regal Books, Ventura, California, 2001. See also James Marcias' chapter "Ego identity and object relations" in *Empirical Perspectives on Object Relations Theory,* edited by J Masling and R F Bornstein, American Psychological Association, Washington DC, United States, 1994.

[15] This, and the following descriptions, taken from www.barna.org, 9/10/01

[16] Op. cit., *Real Teens,* Page 17.

[17] Cited from a report by Sarah Hillman in the *Church Times,* 30 March 2001.

[18] Church groups for young people aged 11 to 14, organised by CPAS, Warwick.

[19] Report in the *Church of England Newspaper,* 1 August 2001.

[20] *Search Engine,* Rev Philip Mounstephen, Bible searches on 10 big issues for 11–14s, from CPAS.

[21] Supported by Children's Forums across Scotland by the Church of Scotland Board of Parish Education, with a regular newsletter called CHOK.

[22] *Youth A Part, Young People and the Church,* National Society, Church House Publishing, 1996.

[23] Article by Viscountess Gill Brentford, "A Window of Opportunity," in *New Directions,* June 1996, Page 8.

[24] Op. cit., (Note 22), Page 75.

[25] Article "Children in focus" by Claire Shelley in the *Church of England Newspaper*, 4 May, 2001, Page 12.

[26] Article "Will your little treasure cost a small fortune?" in *Search, Recent work of the Joseph Rowntree Foundation*, Issue 29, Winter 1997, Page 12.

[27] An Anglican church in Glossop, Derbyshire.

[28] Seminar and discussion hosted by the Southend Bookshop for local clergy, 1 April 2000.

[29] Evidence supplied to the Foresight Ageing Population Panel by Christian Research, 14 August 2000.

The influence of home and family

One summer in the 1940s a small boy was walking with his parents between the Suffolk villages of Bildeston and Wattisham. En route they passed a house with a cat sitting on the wall and the boy stopped to play with the cat, and the parents waited for a few minutes. The cat responded in the way cats do and allowed the boy to tickle him. The parents walked on and simply said, "Catch us up".

The boy played with the cat for many more minutes, and then looking up to see where his parents were, realised they were far up the road. "Wait for me!" he shouted, but to no avail – they were already too far away to hear. He yelled again and again and again, in increasing despair as his parents continued their walk. When the wind was blowing in the right direction he yelled once more with all his might, "Wait for me!" This time the parents heard the faint voice, stopped, looked around and the boy, knowing that they had heard, tore up the road so that he could go with them. I was that boy.

Today, many children find that their parents do not wait for them, as it were, do not really understand them, and however much they may yell, do not share their journey with them, either physically, mentally or spiritually.

Why do Tweenagers trust others?

Family plays a highly important role in the life of Tweenagers. Tweenagers can also be a very lively group with which to live. In 1998, 2.2%, or one family in every 46 which included at least one Tweenager moved house.[1] Moving can disturb relationships, but as this is a third of the percentage of those who move with older teenagers (6.5%) it suggests that Tweenagers enjoy relative stability in their home.

The Focus Groups gave the opportunity to explore not only who young people trust, but why. Responses demonstrated that Tweenagers don't give much thought to why they trust their parents. The one youngster who did not trust his parents had possibly experienced their divorce[2]. Those who did trust their parents could give no substantial reasons for doing so! They gave answers such as, "I've been taught to trust them", "They are always there", "They look after you". However, when it came to trusting other people it was very clear that such trust had to be earned: "Experience has proved I can trust them", "They trust me", "I've known them a long time and they've never let me down."

The participants were asked what would make them stop trusting the people they currently do trust. The answers were again to do with experience:

"If they let me down too many times",

"If they did something really bad which hurt me",

"If they broke my confidences",

"If they told lies which I found out about".

It was important to these Tweenagers to have their trust in others reinforced by good experiences. Correspondingly, it would be a series of bad experiences which would break that trust: one lapse would usually be forgiven and the person given another chance.

Why did they not trust some people? This question produced some fascinating answers, including this selection:

"I don't know them well enough to know if I can trust them."

"Because they manage and control things and make bad things happen."

"I don't trust teachers because they contradict each other."

"I don't trust doctors and nurses because sometimes they do things they said they weren't going to do, or tell you someone isn't going to die and they do."

"I don't trust people on the TV because you don't know what they're really like when they're not on TV."

Overall, they did not trust people whom they did not know, did things they did not like (such as giving out alcohol or drugs), people they perceived (or perhaps were told by parents or teachers) to tell lies – politicians especially came in this bracket but also doctors and nurses, or people who were frequently "angry or horrible".

These factors are a mixture. They show the values which this age-group is beginning to form, such as a dislike of alcohol and drugs, or the perceived importance that public figures should be honest and not "make bad things happen". The other part of the mixture is relationships – if they don't know people they are unlikely to trust them. Is this perhaps part of the reason why non-church-going youngsters do not trust church leaders, they just do not know them?

There were some worrying responses when these Tweenagers were asked what people they do not trust would have to do be trusted. Most of them did not expect people they did not now trust to be able to do anything which would win their trust in the future. The only positive answer was that it would help if they got to know them and found out that, after all, they were "nice to you".

This Focus Group exploration was one of the most important. Although it did not specifically delve into trust in church or in God, it showed that young people needed to know a person before they would trust them, and that their experiences of what that person does must be positive. This is a very post-modern attitude: trust must be earned, and continue to be earned. It contrasts with the old attitude of trusting a person because of their position or because you were told to.

In a project looking at 10 to 14 year olds in the Church of Scotland[3], youth workers working with this age group particularly made it clear that the relationship with churchgoing young people is crucial. It is only if that relationship is good and the young people trust their leaders that they will come to Christian activities, listen to what is taught, be willing to talk about it with their leaders, and thus grow in their Christian faith.

This reveals how vitally important it is to build relationships with this age-group if they are ever to be touched with the Gospel and have the opportunity to develop the most important relationship of all, with God himself. Perhaps it reinforces the need for churches to have *Children's* Workers (as opposed to Youth Workers working with older teenagers), that is, those who will so work with this age-group that they will come to be trusted.

The post-modern importance of "relationship, belonging and community, areas that the church has neglected"[4] (as one researcher put it) can immediately be seen here. So can the implications which she then highlighted, stressing the priority of "principle over pro-gramme", that is, where trust is built up commitment will follow. It is this, rather than particular events, which retain young people.

Parents are in!

Those in the sample were asked who they trusted. The list below shows parents and other family members are the people they trust most, followed by medical personnel and the police. No other groups were trusted by a majority of Tweenagers.

Table 2.1: People whom Tweenagers trust and distrust

Person TOP 6	YES, trust %	Person MIDDLE 5	YES, trust %	Person BOTTOM 6	YES, trust %
Parents	89	ChildLine	35	Guide/Scout leaders	19
Other family members	71	Other children and young people	34	Social workers	17
Doctors & nurses	59	Youth club leaders	32	Lawyers	14
Police	56	Churchgoers	31	People on TV	7
Teachers	44	A neighbour	29	Politicians	5
Church leaders	42			Journalists	3

Parents, other family members, ChildLine, other young people and youth club leaders were trusted *whatever the Tweenager's age.*

However, the level of trust in the last four of the top six declined with age, as Figure 2.2 shows, although it still remains higher than for the next group. The levels of trust changed most sharply between those aged 11 and 12, that is during the important first year or two of secondary school.

Figure 2.2: Tweenager trust in four key groups by age

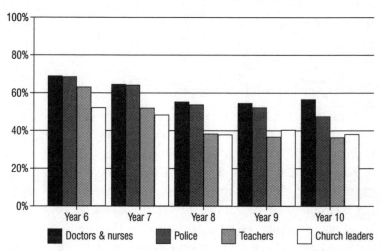

The level of trust did not vary by gender, though boys were marginally more likely to trust parents than girls (90% to 88%). Girls, however, trusted ChildLine significantly more than boys (42% to 27%), which is perhaps why more than three-quarters, 78%, of the calls made to ChildLine are from girls.[5]

Generally the higher the grades they usually obtained, the greater the level of trust. Thus, for example, 94% of those who usually got A grades trusted their parents, 90% of those getting Bs, 85% of those getting Cs, and 76% of those getting Ds, Es or Fs.

The difference church makes

Does the trust young people have in the "top six" groups vary at all by whether they go to church? Table 2.3 shows a positive answer.

Table 2.3: Trust in key groups by churchgoing

Do you trust ...?	Regular %	Occasional %	Lapsed %	Never %	Overall %
Parents	94	92	88	87	89
Family members	77	70	67	70	71
Doctors & nurses	67	56	58	52	59
Police	69	56	54	44	56
Teachers	55	45	41	33	44
Church leaders	72	41	31	13	42

Churchgoing improves your trust! Not just in God but also your trust in other people as well, even such important people as your parents. No doubt this will encourage parents! The differences in Table 2.3 are striking, with regular churchgoers clearly exhibiting greater trust in all key groups of people (and in others also, although not shown in this Table). While the differentials in the bottom line about church leaders could be expected, the differences on other lines are also substantial. It is important such trust does not lead to unwittingly trusting those who are a danger to young people.

Findings in the Focus Groups were similar: everyone in the churchgoing group trusted their parents, but one of the non-church-goers did not. The participants were asked specifically whether they trusted their friends (which the questionnaire did not ask) and in both groups trust in friends came second, though it was important for more of the non-churchgoers than the churchgoers. In another project looking at Gen Xers[6] (18 to 35 year-olds), participants in Focus Groups were very reluctant to choose between their trust in and the importance of family and friends. Friends are an increasingly important factor in life as young people grow up.

After parents and friends, both Focus Groups followed the same pattern as the questionnaire respondents: other family members next, then doctors and nurses, police and teachers. Interestingly only two of the churchgoers and none of the non-churchgoers said they trusted church leaders! Responses about those they least trusted were slightly different to the questionnaire results, with people on TV coming out worst followed equally by politicians and neighbours, then leaders of Guides or Scouts, social workers and youth club leaders.

Is this because the exercise of trusting God develops a person's ability to trust, as it were? Or is it because the security of trusting God gives a belief in His omnipotence which allows greater trust to be given to people generally? Or perhaps because respecting people as God's creation makes it easier to trust them?

Three Tweenagers in every seven, 42%, said they trusted church leaders. While not all of these had been to a church, how did their trust vary by denomination for those who had? Numbers in some denominations were too few to give reliable percentages.

- 50% of Baptist Tweeenagers trusted their leaders
- 43% Anglican
- 42% Methodist, and
- 36% Church leaders of other denominations.

Religious commitment and churchgoing

A more specific question (Question 17) asked about present religious commitment. How does commitment measure against churchgoing? This is explored in Table 2.4, which is based on a total of 2,047 replies from those answering both questions.

Table 2.4: Tweenagers' religious commitment by regularity of churchgoing

	Certain Christian %	Unsure Christian %	Lapsed Christian %	Never Christian %	Another religion %	Total %
Regular	30	6	0	0	0	36
Occasional	10	5	0	2	1	18
Lapsed	9	7	2	3	1	22
Never	6	6	1	9	2	24
Total	55	24	3	14	4	100

The majority of Christian Tweenagers say they go to church regularly (that is 30% out of the 55% who are Christian), and a further 18% (10% of 55%) go occasionally. Note, however, that there are some Christian Tweenagers who never go to church, and presumably find their Christian nurture and encouragement elsewhere (in Sunday School or youth clubs?), or who have a different definition of "Christian" from the others.

Those who are not sure if they are Christian are evenly spread across the categories of churchgoing. Those no longer a Christian understandably no longer go to church or have never been, and the majority of those who have never been a Christian have never been to church. There are a small number of Tweenagers, 42 in total in this sample (2%), who have never been a Christian but who nevertheless go to church occasionally. Those who belong to another religion do not go to a Christian church, although 20 in this sample, 1%, say they go occasionally, perhaps for school events or parades of Guides or Scouts.

The difference religious commitment makes

The difference religious commitment, as opposed to churchgoing, makes to a Tweenager's trust in key groups of people is shown next.

Table 2.5: Trust in key groups of people by religious commitment

	Certain Christian %	Unsure Christian %	Lapsed Christian %	Never Christian %	Another religion %	Overall %
Parents	93	88	73	87	94	89
Other family	76	69	54	69	64	71
GPs, nurses	65	56	44	49	58	59
Police	65	53	33	43	45	56
Teachers	52	39	29	29	43	44
Church leaders	59	34	15	13	16	42

This again shows that those with a specific Christian commitment have a higher degree of trust than those who are unsure or have none. Those who are "no longer a Christian" have the lowest percentages of trust in others. The Table also shows that those belonging to another religion likewise have a high degree of trust.

Although the figures in the "another religion" column are lower than those in the "Certain I'm a Christian" column, the actual numbers of young people responding who belonged to other religions was only 4%, and these percentages therefore have a wider range of error associated with them. The conclusion that Christianity leads to a higher degree of trust than other faiths cannot be drawn from these figures. In any case the final figure in the "another religion" column, 16%, would appear to have been answered about church leaders rather than imams, rabbis or like leaders of other religions.

Tables 2.3 and 2.5 show that whether it is religious practice or religious commitment which is considered, either makes a real impact on Tweenagers' ability to trust key groups of people in their lives[7].

Divorce and its outcomes

Parents are shown to be the most trusted group of people in a Tweenager's world. Unfortunately that trust is sometimes shattered.

In the late 1990s the number of divorces in the UK was about 160,000 per year[8], a relatively static number because the number of marriages is decreasing and the extent of cohabitation rapidly rising. Cohabitees who separate obviously do not divorce.

Many, though not all, divorcing couples have children. Again for the last five years of the 20th century the number of children affected by their parents divorce has been relatively constant at 175,000 children a year under the age of 16. If the number of children affected and the number of divorces were constant over 15 years almost a quarter of all children's parents would divorce before their 16th birthday. In 2000 there were 2.5 million children living with step-parents in the UK. Of children whose parents divorce,

- 28% are under 5
- 44% are aged 5 to 10, and
- 28% are aged 11 to 15.[9]

One Tweenager in 16 will experience their parents' separation and divorce. A study from Northern Ireland in 1991 showed that Christian divorces were only at half the rate of non-Christian.[10] If this were true across the UK, and also still true ten years later, one churchgoing Tweenager in 32 would experience their parents' divorce. But both elements are likely to have changed, and probably a more realistic figure is one church Tweenager in 20 per year will experience parental separation. How many is that in your church?

A large survey of 13 to 15 year olds found that young Christians believed "divorce is acceptable"[11]. Thus answered 82% of those who were Church of England (and 58% of Muslims).[12]

The impact of such trauma on children generally and Tweenagers in particular varies. A detailed study of children who experienced parental separation and life in step-families by a team from King's College, London, supported by the Joseph Rowntree Foundation[13], found that:

- A quarter of the children whose parents had separated said no one talked to them about the separation when it happened. Only 5% said they were given full explanations and a chance to ask questions. Most reported that they were confused and distressed by the separation.
- Grandparents and friends were children's key confidants in the weeks following separation; confiding in fathers and siblings was rare.
- Children who felt close to their maternal grandparents had fewer adjustment problems. No such association was found for closeness to paternal grandparents.
- Children who felt they had poor relationships with their parents, and those more involved in conflict between parents and step-parents, tended to have more adjustment problems.
- Over half the children who lived in two households because of separated parents were positive about their "divided" lives. Those who had an active role in decisions about these arrangements, and those able to talk to their parents about problems concerning their "divided" lives were likely to have positive feelings about moving between households.

However, one in five children in step-families fail to cope with the new relationship and run away.[14] 77,000 children run away from home each year. By the age of 16, one in nine has run away from home, with 14% spending more than a week away from home. Most runaways are Tweenagers between 13 and 15, though a quarter run away before the age of 11. Why do they flee? Because of family arguments, physical abuse or sibling rivalry. Others go after being bullied at school or having bad experiences linked to drugs or alcohol.[15]

Note the importance of grandparents. The claim by one periodical "that this generation of grandparents isn't pulling its weight in looking after the children"[16] is not always true whatever the parents may say, especially when trouble brews. Grandparental stability, wisdom and influence pervades.

The same organisation, the Joseph Rowntree Trust, one of the major British research agencies, has shown that children of separated families have a higher probability of:

- Living in poverty and poor housing
- Being poorer when they are adults
- Behavioural problems
- Performing less well in school
- Needing medical treatment
- Leaving home/school when young
- Becoming sexually active, pregnant, or parent at an early age
- Depressive symptoms, high levels of smoking and drinking, and drug use during adolescence and adulthood.[17]

What are the factors affecting the outcomes? The report states:
- Financial hardship can limit educational achievement
- Family conflict before, during and after separation can contribute to behavioural problems
- Parental ability to recover from distress of separation affects children's ability to adjust
- Multiple changes in family structure increase the probability of poor outcomes
- Quality contact with the non-resident parent can improve outcomes.[18]

Similar findings are evidenced in other countries also. A North American report indicated that children do not always make the connection between parental violence and marriage break-up ("to them, it appears that Mom or Dad has gone mad"), often feel guilty, suffer acute loneliness, and struggle to adjust to parents' second marriage.[19] Other research indicates that there are also ethnic differences in the outcomes.[20]

A related topic is poverty itself. Over one-third of British children officially live in poverty[21] – of itself, an appalling statistic. Only a little is known about the effect this has on children's understanding of the economic world, or their own behaviour, beliefs and aspirations.[22] Some research would suggest that poverty as such impinges less on young people than the general social and economic climate[23].

Another related topic is that of parental authority, especially in cases of breakdown. The survey did not examine this issue as it has been explored elsewhere.[24] At least one headmaster, Neil Thornley, Head of Fearns High School, Bacup, Lancashire, believes "special early intervention is needed for dysfunctional families".[25]

Not all single adults living with children have been divorced, and the phrase "single parent" no longer implies such (if it ever did). How churches welcome single parents, Christian or not yet Christian, is often crucial to the church's well-being. It is also often crucial for the single parents themselves[26].

What is a family?

The survey asked Tweenagers how they would define a family. Four definitions were offered from which they could choose. They replied:

56% Any person or group whom you love or care about deeply, or who love or care about you deeply

37% Where all members of the family are related to each other by birth, adoption or marriage

4% Any group of people who live in the same home together

3% Any group of people who share the same set of values and goals in life.

These percentages did not vary by school year or gender, but they did by the grade a child usually obtained, as given in Table 2.6. This shows that the normally accepted "birth/marriage" definition, here in number two position, was accepted most by those who get C grades, and the "love" definition, in number one position, is the more accepted the greater the school grade of the respondent. The "group" definitions, the last two listed above, are accepted much more by those getting lower grades than those getting higher grades. This indicates that the classic meaning of "family" is in jeopardy.

Table 2.6: Definition of a family by school grade

	A %	B %	C %	D–F %	Overall %
People who love/care deeply	61	56	46	41	56
Where all are related by birth or marriage	34	38	41	31	37
Any group who live in same home	3	4	7	16	4
Any group who share same values	2	2	6	12	3

What is "home"?

Tweenagers were asked to indicate which one of five statements best described their home. Each began, "My home is a place where..."

    59% I feel secure and loved

    24% Sometimes I feel loved, other times I don't

     9% Each of us is *trying* to love each other

     4% I usually feel uncomfortable: I would rather be elsewhere

     4% I feel comfortable though we are not a close, loving family

These answers did not vary by school year or gender either, but again they did by usual school grade, given in Table 2.7:

Table 2.7: Definition of home by school grade

	A %	B %	C %	D–F %	Overall %
I feel secure and loved	66	59	50	29	59
Sometimes I feel loved	19	25	27	29	24
Trying to love each other	9	8	7	21	9
Would rather be elsewhere	3	4	8	9	4
Comfortable, but not close	3	4	8	12	4

This Table demonstrates similar resonance to the previous one, except that those with higher school grades are more likely to affirm the expected first answer. But the last two categories, in which home is not as welcoming as it might be, are affirmed by more than a fifth of those with lowest school grades. Despite the similarity of answers to these questions, there was no significant correlation between them. Could the fact that those with lower grades are giving answers of home being where they are uncomfortable, or comfortable but not close, be a reflection that these are Tweens who have divorced parents?

The next Table shows how the answers about home vary by religious commitment.

Table 2.8: Definition of home by religious commitment

	Certain Christian %	Unsure Christian %	Lapsed Christian %	Never Christian %	Another religion %	*Overall* %
Secure & loved	65	55	43	50	56	**59**
Sometimes loved	19	28	38	30	27	**24**
Trying to love	8	9	9	7	8	**9**
Want to be away	4	4	4	8	4	**9**
Comfy, not close	4	4	6	5	5	**4**
Overall	**59**	**24**	**9**	**4**	**4**	***100***

This Table illustrates again what emerged earlier: those who are Christian or who belong to another religion are likely to feel more secure, while those who have given up Christianity seem to have given up with that some of their security. Or perhaps they lost their security because their parents divorced, and in the process gave up their Christianity. Unfortunately it is not possible to discover from this survey which was the cause and which the effect.

The real variations are in the first two rows in Table 2.8; the changes in the final three rows are of little consequence.

The ideal family

In the Focus Groups the question was asked "What would your ideal family be like?", and answers fell into several groups:

- The make-up of the family. Several would like a sister or a brother ("a big brother who would stick up for me"), or a younger brother or sister rather than an older one, or "a brother to play sport with".
- Attitudes, especially of parents. "Parents that let you do what you want", "Parents who are loving and caring", "Everyone being nice; people who don't get annoyed with you".
- Possessions. The possibility of having rich parents was very popular, along with the things that could then be purchased – a football season ticket, a big house and garden, or exotic pets were all mentioned.

One factor brought up in both groups was that the ideal family would be 'fun', but quite what that means in practice they had difficulty identifying. This came up again in relation to friends, and it seems that 'fun' is recognisable when you are experiencing it but hard to define.

When asked whether they thought they would be able to create such a family when they grew up, they were much more realistic. "It's not possible, kids always argue and I'm sure mine would", "When I grow up I'm likely to be the same as my own Mum and Dad so it wouldn't be very different". This age group, while dreaming of what they might like to be or have, are beginning to realise that in life things do not usually work out that way.

Passing on the faith

How then in the context of one's home, where three-fifths, 59%, of Tweenagers feel secure and loved, may the Christian faith best be communicated? There are many books[27] and articles on this topic. For example, one American author suggests:[28]

- Pray for God's wisdom and guidance.
- Learn to interpret negatives. When your child says, "I hate school," find out why, with the aim of turning all negatives into positives.

- Make mealtimes positive. Take opportunities to express thankfulness not only for food but also for good things happening at the time. Avoid criticism, but allow humour, positive conversations, and questions like "What was the best part of your day today?"
- Use family prayer and Bible times to overcome negativity.
- Watch out for negative versus positive influences in your kids' lives. Be aware of the music and friends that influence them negatively, and work to give your kids positive experiences and memories.
- Be a positive model for your children.

An article in the *Daily Telegraph* emphasised that family meals were making a comeback, with a survey showing that three-quarters of families eat together at least once a week. This was based on studying 800 families over a three month period in 2000. "More than 80% of parents felt that family dinners were a vital part of home life."[29] It is part of what another author wrote of giving them "a little undivided time"[30].

An Australian author, emphasising that all young people have access to God's Spirit, says that their spirituality is shaped through transactions:

- With the natural world
- With human artefacts
- With their culture
- With social environments
- With other individuals
- With words and ideas, and by providential care experienced in life events.[31]

One British Baptist minister undertook research of Manse Children, and found that just over half, 51%, had a whole hearted commitment to the Christian faith many years later, and a further sixth, 18%, a "warm" commitment. This is encouraging news, although as he points out his research is based on children who are now adult, rather than on current children for whom the outcome may be different.[32]

Erica Brown wrote a paper on the care of dying children. Some of the points she makes are also valid for children in a wider circle of experiences. She emphasised that young teens need to have:

- Opportunities to express their fears for themselves and for family members
- Privacy, especially when undergoing personal care
- Opportunities to maintain autonomy and independence for as long as possible
- Support from peer groups as well as family members
- Involvement in decisions regarding their care
- Maintenance of familiar cultural and religious traditions.[33]

Parenting models

Table 2.9: Different family styles

PARENTING MODELS

Permissive	Authoritative	Authoritarian
• Stresses support	• Stresses control	• Stresses control
• NO control	• AND support	• NOT supportive

PARENT-TEEN RELATIONSHIP MODELS

Extreme Affection	Companionship	Extreme Control
• Suffocating affection	• Open communication	• Little emotional
• Youth afraid indepen-	between parents	connection between
dence will hurt parent	and children	generations
• Poor communication	• Fair discipline	
with strong discipline		

FAMILY TYPE

Transparent	Translucent	Opaque
• Family has no	• Family is integrated	• Family completely
differences from	with society but	separate from society
general social values	has own distinctions	• Family is right; all
• Parents offer no	• Parents interpret	outside sources are
interpretation of the	outside world fairly	"fallen" or evil
outside world	• Family is not hostile	• Family ascribes faith
• Family has no	to other values	only to those who
distinctive values		fully conform

Parenting Tweenagers is a complex task, and there have been different ways of trying to analyse it. The Table on the previous page gives three models, and some of the attitudes within each. Research has shown that those family styles which are closest to those in the middle column "will consistently have greater success in ensuring their adolescent children maintain the essentials of the family's religious values"[34].

Irrespective of parenting style, some things are universally important. The ten things every child, and Tweenager, longs to hear are[35]:

- I love you   • You did that so well   • I'm so proud of you
- Well done!   • You did your very best   • You are a great kid
- I trust you   • You said that so clearly   • You make my day
- I just love to have you around.

Have your own room?

One part of "home" is whether or not a Tweenager has his/her own room. In this study, 84% reported that they did, five in every six. Somewhat surprisingly perhaps, this percentage did not vary by age, gender or other control factors, most likely because it varies by the number of siblings and the size of house parents can afford.

The remainder shared with their brothers or sisters. It is reported, however, that "teens who share a bedroom with a sibling learn better negotiating skills than a teen with his/her own room who spends a lot of time there. Sharing a bedroom could result in relationships that last longer and marriages that are more stable."[36]

The tradition of churchgoing

The Tweenagers were asked if they knew whether their parents or grandparents had ever gone to church. 13% didn't know about their parents, 24% didn't know about their maternal grandparents, and 31% about their paternal grandparents. These replies are ignored in the following Table, with scores grossed up to compensate.

Table 2.10: Churchgoing of parents and grandparents

Churchgoing frequency	Parents %	Maternal Grandparents %	Paternal Grandparents %
Regular	33	32	33
Occasional	22	29	26
Never	15	13	19
Lapsed	14	17	14
One parent only	14	8	7
Recently started	2	1	1

Table 2.10 shows that there is remarkably little difference between the churchgoing habits of parents and grandparents, except fewer parents go occasionally and more parents are "split", with one going and the other not. A few have recently started going to church, but about 1 in every 7, 14%, used to go but has now stopped. A third of parents and grandparents go regularly.

This similarity between grandparental and parental churchgoing is not a new finding. It was shown in a study in 1981 by Dr Robert Towler[37], and for evangelical (but not liberal) children by Professor David Martin.[38]

As might be expected the percentages in Table 2.10 vary with a Tweenager's own churchgoing behaviour and their religious commitment, though they do not vary by their gender or age.

There are two ways of looking at this interaction – what Tweenagers do now and how that meshes with what their parents do, or what the parents do and how that meshes with what the Tweenager does. It is this latter which is perhaps more interesting since it shows how the Tweenager now acts in the light of parental example. Accordingly, Table 2.11 shows the churchgoing habits of Tweenagers by what their parents do. Table A4/3 in Appendix 4 gives the reverse – what parents are doing and what their Tweenagers are doing. The conclusion is that parental example is critical for young people's church involvement.

It is also possible to look at the same issue by Tweenage religious commitment rather than churchgoing. Although these two are correlated, they are not the same. Both are given in Appendix 4 also, as Tables A4/4 and A4/5. The highest figures in each vertical column have been highlighted, and show a clear pattern.

This is an important Table, showing that **Tweenagers follow their parents' example.** Thus:

- A majority of Tweenagers regularly attend church where both their parents either have always gone (five-sixths, 83%, of Tweenagers in this case), or where one parent attends (56%), or where the parents have recently started (54%), perhaps through their young people's example, or they have started to go and have taken their children with them.

Table 2.11: Churchgoing habits of parents and Tweenagers

	Tweenagers				
Parents	Regular %	Occasional %	Lapsed %	Never %	Base
Regular	83	9	6	2	534
Occasional	15	37	27	21	346
Lapsed	11	20	49	20	224
Never	6	10	23	61	238
One parent only	56	24	17	3	225
Recently started	54	21	13	12	24
Overall	*36*	*18*	*22*	*24*	1,591

- Just over a third, 37%, of Tweenagers whose parents attend church occasionally do the same, twice the overall percentage
- Half the Tweenagers, 49%, who have stopped going to church, have parents who do the same
- Three-fifths, 61%, of Tweenagers who have never gone to church have parents who have never gone, either.

The boxes highlighted in Table A4/3 are the same as those highlighted here for the top four categories. In other words, they are telling a consistent story.

How typical are these answers?

The above findings are important. How far are they replicated in other research? An analysis of children's churchgoing in Switzerland in 1990 related to their parents' churchgoing is reported in *Religious Trends* No 3[39]. The figures for those who don't go to church are virtually identical to those in Table 2.11 for "those who have never gone". The Swiss percentages are, respectively, 4%, 15% and 81% against those in Table 2.10 of 6%, 10% and 84% (adding the last two columns together).

However, other findings do not follow the Swiss pattern quite so well[40]. The implication behind the figures is similar, however: parents who go to church irregularly are likely to have children who go irregularly or not at all.

For those who are regular churchgoers, the Swiss study gives a different picture. Their figures for the top line in Table 2.11 are 33%, 41% and 26%, implying that parents who go regularly are most likely to have children who go irregularly. The very high first percentage in Table 2.11, 74%, suggests that in the UK, parents who go to church are most likely to have children who go regularly.

Figures from an earlier European source[41], however, confirm the findings of Table 2.11 almost exactly. They show that 66% of churchgoing parents are likely to have churchgoing children, 17% nominal children (or "occasional attenders"), and 17% non-churchgoing children, which are very close to the 74%, 14% and 12% of Table 2.11. They also show that 26% of nominal parents are likely to have regular churchgoing children, 44% nominal children and 30% non-churchgoing children, akin to the 15%, 37% and 48% of Table 2.11. Of non-churchgoing parents, 10% had regular churchgoing children, 18% nominal, and 72% non-churchgoing, comparing with 6%, 10% and 84%, a much closer comparison.

These two examples, the only ones known to this author, show a degree of similarity in findings between Table 2.11 and other studies of regular churchgoing parents and non-churchgoing parents. It is in the middle category, measured with different words in all three studies, that the main differences lie.

These results are important for at least two other reasons. Firstly, families and children going to church help build family life, but they also help build the church. The image of families and children attending church draws other families along as well. When discussing the future of the church in a roadshow in Bath[42], those present made it clear that the reason people had joined their church in the previous five years was because it was a friendly church and because families and children came also.

Secondly, Grace Davie, senior lecturer in sociology in the University of Exeter, has shown that parents have a greater religiousness than couples without children[43], suggesting "parenting encourages religious responses. The family itself becomes an important site for the handing on of religious memory, *the more so in its traditional forms*"[44].

Churchgoing of grandparents

The Tweenager survey also asked about grandparents' churchgoing. Table 2.12 gives the equivalent figures to those in Table 2.11 for maternal grandparents, and Table A4/6 for paternal grandparents. Although the study differentiated between the two sets, the results were identical whichever side of the family grandparents represented.

Table 2.12: Churchgoing of maternal grandparents and Tweenagers

	Tweenagers				
Maternal grandparents	*Regular* %	*Occasional* %	*Lapsed* %	*Never* %	*Base*
Regular	61	18	15	6	429
Occasional	33	20	24	23	391
Lapsed	32	22	26	20	226
Never	25	12	19	44	178
One parent only	47	20	20	13	112
Recently started	40	16	20	24	25
Overall	36	18	22	24	1,361

Tables 2.12 and A4/6 are similar to Table 2.11 except for the two lines "go occasionally" and "lapsed". The answers given here do not vary significantly from the overall answers in the bottom line, showing that grandparents' occasional or ceased churchgoing has not influenced their Tweenage grandchildren. However, regular churchgoing, either singly or as a couple, or non-churchgoing has been replicated in their grandchildren.

In other words, going regularly or not at all, is part of the family tradition, as it were, and the grandchildren have followed this example. It is where churchgoing was, or had become, intermittent that the example had less impact on the second generation. This finding is similar to the one related to parental churchgoing – regular or non-attendance has an influence, the occasional does not.

This Chapter shows ...

- Parents and other family members are trusted by most Tweenagers, nine in ten. This "greatest trust" remained true throughout the age of a Tweenager, even though overall trust levels fell as Tweenagers became older. The higher the school grades of Tweenagers the more likely they are to trust their parents and family. Churchgoing parents were trusted slightly more than non-churchgoing parents.
- Three Tweenagers in every seven, 42%, trusted church leaders, Baptists more than those of other denominations.
- Trust is based on relationship and experience. Tweenagers trust people they know and who have proved themselves worthy of such trust. Winning trust if it does not exist is difficult, and probably only possible by getting to know the untrusted.
- Religious commitment and regular churchgoing do not always go hand in hand for Tweenagers: more than half who say they are Christian also say they attend regularly and a further third occasionally, but a quarter never or no longer go to church.
- Tweenagers who are no longer Christian have not only given up regular church attendance but are also likely to have less trust in their parents or other societal leaders. It would seem that in giving up their faith, they give up also in some of their other relationships, or vice versa. They also tended to feel less secure at home.
- Those of religions other than Christianity are very similar to Christians in regularity of commitment and levels of trust in others. Faith appears to deepen relationships irrespective of the religion of that faith.
- Divorce hits young people hard, although this aspect was not explicitly part of the Tweenager survey.
- The majority of respondents opted for a definition of "family" which concentrated on people loving each other, rather than the traditional definition of blood relationship.

- Home was where Tweens felt "loved and secure". This was less true for those with less academic success where people *trying* to love each other dominated, or living together but not feeling close. Could these results reflect the divorce of their parents?
- Five Tweenagers in six, 84%, had their own room at home.
- Tweenagers tended to follow their parents' example if they were regular churchgoers, or if they never went to church. Where only one parent went to church, this example was still largely reflected in Tweenager attendance. It was the same for grandparents too. These findings are replicated in other, earlier, research.
- Tweenagers also followed parental example when parents had given up going to church (Tweenagers largely had also) or when parents only went occasionally (Tweenagers only went occasionally also). Other research did not replicate this finding so positively.

NOTES

[1] *Social Focus on Young People,* National Statistics, The Stationery Office, 2000, Table 1.4.

[2] This was not specifically asked in the public setting of a group.

[3] *Ministry among Young People,* Survey among ministers and lay people in the Church of Scotland, Board of Parish Education, Church of Scotland, Christian Research report, London, January 2001.

[4] Research report, *Reaching and Keeping the Postmodern Generation,* Jenna McCormack, June 2002, Page 17.

[5] *ChildLine has now helped a million children* leaflet, ChildLine, 1999, 0800 1111

[6] *Generation X: Attitudes and Lifestyle,* Christian and non-Christian, Research Report for the Evangelical Alliance and project partners, Christian Research, London, March 2001.

[7] Conversely, it could be argued that those who have an ability to trust are more likely to have religious practice or commitment.

[8] *Population Trends,* National Statistics, The Stationery Office, No 104, Summer 2001, Table 2.1.

[9] *Religious Trends No 2, 2000/2001,* edited Peter Brierley, HarperCollins and Christian Research, London, 1999, Table 4.7.4.

[10] Article "Religion in Northern Ireland", *Irish Christian Handbook 1995/96,* Christian Research, London, 1994, edited by Peter Brierley and Boyd Myers, Table 4, Page 24.

[11] Article "Young Christians back unmarried sex" by Victoria Coombe, in the *Daily Telegraph,* 14 March 2001, on publication of the book *The Fourth R for the Third Millennium* by Revd Prof Leslie Francis.

[12] The article also stated that a large majority, 85%, of Roman Catholics did not believe that sex outside marriage was wrong (as did 51% of Muslims).

[13] Article "Children's views of their changing families", *Findings*, Joseph Rowntree Foundation, September 2001, www.jrf.org.uk

[14] Article "Runaways on the Increase" by Jill Sherman in *The Times*, 23 March 2001, and quoted in the *R Briefing*, Issue 34, June 2001, Page 3.

[15] Ibid.

[16] Article by Nicholas Coleridge, *The Spectator*, 3 August 2002.

[17] Article "Divorce and separation: the outcomes for children", *Foundations*, Joseph Rowntree Foundation, York, June 1998.

[18] Ibid., but also article "Splitting the difference" by Polly Toynbee, *Search*, Recent work of the Joseph Rowntree Foundation, Issue 30, Summer 1998, Page 5.

[19] *Second Chances*, Wallerstein and Blakeslee, Ticknor and Fields, New York, 1989, and quoted in *Context*, July 1992, Volume 2, Number 2, Page 2.

[20] See, for example, the research reported in articles in *Youth and Society*, Sage Periodicals Press, Volume 26, Number 3, March 1995.

[21] That is to say, the income of the household to which they belong is less than the minimum "liveable income" set by the Government.

[22] See, for example, article "Small expectations" by Decca Aitkenhead in *Search*, recent work of the Joseph Rowntree Foundation, York, Issue 32, Summer 1999, Pages 12 to 15.

[23] Article "The impact of poverty on children's lives" by Francis McGlone, *Family Policy*, Autumn 2000, Page 7.

[24] A brief article on the topic is "The chicken or the egg: families, children and authority" by Rosalind Bayley in *Family Policy Bulletin*, Family Policy Studies Centre, Winter 1997/98, Page 2.

[25] Ibid.

[26] One helpful Christian book on this topic is *Single Parents in Focus*, Tom Beardshaw, Guy Hordern and Christine Tufnell, Care for the Family, Cardiff, 2000.

[27] A useful book, of wider scope than this issue, is *Touching the Future*, Rev Gill Dallow, The Bible Reading Fellowship, Oxford, 2002. One American book available through St Mary's Press in Dublin is *Passing on the Faith*, a radical new model for youth and family ministry, by Merton Strommen and Richard Hardel, 2000.

[28] Article "Positive parenting" by Bob Hostetler in *Living with Teenagers*, Nav Press, United States, August 2000, Volume 22, Number 11, Pages 14–16, available through www.navpres.com/ctt

[29] Article "Family mealtimes are back" by Nicole Martin, *Daily Telegraph*, 3 April 2001.

[30] Article "Taking time to shape the gems" by Feryl Harris, *Ministry*, Nampa, United States, March 2000, Page 24.

[31] Article "Children and spirituality, passing on faith to our children" by Glenn Cupit, *Zadok Perspectives*, Number 56, Autumn 1997, Pages 12–15.

[32] *Manse Children*, Some indicators towards their faith, Rev C K Sykes, October, 2000, details available from revkensykes@netscape.net

[33] Article, "How Long is the Future?" by Erica Brown, Implicit Religion, *Journal of the Centre for the Study of Implicit Religion and Contemporary Spirituality*, Middlesex University, Volume 3, Number 1, May 2000, Pages 5–13.

[34] Taken from an article "An effective parenting mix" in *Context,* MARC Canada, Ontario, Volume 3, Number 1, 1993, Page 2.

[35] Article "A sense of value" by Peter Meadows in *Care for the Family* magazine, Cardiff, Summer 2001, Page 13.

[36] Article in *Time* magazine, 9 October, 2000, Page 116.

[37] Leeds Common Religion Survey, Dr Robert Towler, 1981. Basic frequencies published by Helen Krarup, Leeds University, September 1984.

[38] Article "Age and sex variations of church attenders" by Professor David Martin, *Prospects for the Eighties,* Bible Society, London, 1980, Page 12.

[39] *Religious Trends* No 3, 2002/2003, Christian Research, London, 2001, Table 1.6, quoting from an article "The demographic characteristics of linguistic and religious groups in Switzerland" by Werner Haug and Philippe Wanner of the Federal Statistical Office, Neuchâtel in Volume 2 Population Studies No 31, *The demographic characteristics of national minorities in certain European states,* edited by Werner Haug and others, published by the Council of Europe Directorate General III, Social Cohesion, Strasbourg, January 2000.

[40] The Swiss figures for "irregularity", presumably equivalent to "occasional" in Table 2.11, are 8%, 61%, and 31% against the 15%, 37% and 48% in Table 2.11, but the latter is more detailed being split between "stopping" and "not going" so the comparison is not exact.

[41] *Young People and Values in Western Europe,* Pro Mundi Vita Dossiers, April 1984, and given in *Children and the Church,* MARC Monograph No 16, Peter Brierley, January 1989.

[42] Presenting the results of the English Church Attendance Survey in association with Youth For Christ, Scripture Union and the Church Pastoral Aid Society, one of 10 Roadshows, Bath, 10 March 2000.

[43] *Religion in Modern Europe,* A Memory Mutates, Dr Grace Davie, Oxford University Press, Oxford, 2000, Page 68.

[44] Ibid., italics mine.

The impact of school

Socrates knew! He wrote: "Children today are tyrants. They contradict their parents, gobble their food and tyrannise their teachers."[1] Some things never change!

Andy Hickford was the youth leader of a large Luton church in the 1990s. He realised this "meant entering the world of the teenager and making Jesus real... we soon discovered that a teenager's world revolved around school and family."[2] Others today, like Lee Jackson, Head of Leeds Faith in Schools, would doubtless agree. So what kind of school do young people like?

A good school

The Guardian ran a competition in the summer of 2001 asking young people what kind of school they would like. This is what they said. "The school we'd like is...

- Beautiful
- Comfortable
- Safe
- Listening
- Flexible
- Relevant
- Respectful
- Without walls
- For everybody."[3]

Is that how they might describe the church they would like? A "comfortable school" would have "cushions on the floors, blinds that keep out the sun and quiet rooms where we can chill out"[4]. The last is interesting. One fast growing New Church in north west Kent started some after-school clubs for Tweenagers and those younger. They offered a tuck shop, a homework room, a recreation and sports facility, etc., and a "quiet room", and which was used by many young people. Kenilworth Youth for Christ run a lunch time chill room, where young people go to listen to ambient music, take time out to be quiet or chat if they need to. This has proved very popular.

A "listening school" included having "children on the governing body"[5]. Having representative children in positions of authority has emerged in other contexts as important for young people. For example, one reason why some Catholic Tweenagers stay on in church is because a few of them help as altar servers. One of the practical outcomes suggested from the English Church Attendance Survey was that churches could try and have 35% of their governing council filled by those under 35 – including maybe some younger people.

A "relevant school" was one where young people learned "through experience, experiments and exploration". Could Sunday Schools accept such a challenge? A "school without walls" was where young people could "go outside to learn".

A "respectful school" was one "where we are not treated as empty vessels to be filled with information, but where teachers treat us as individuals." A "school for everybody" meant a mix of young people from all backgrounds and abilities. (Presumably that would include children who have been excluded in their primary school, 62% of whom do not offend again.[6])

These characteristics show the type of learning environment where young people would feel comfortable. Finding a different environment in a church may be so off-putting that their ability to learn what is being shared may be impaired.

Bullying

By a "safe school" these young people essentially meant somewhere that is emotionally safe, where all their friends are[7], and where they are safe from bullying. While doubtless there has always been some bullying at school, it seems to have increased in both the number of incidents and the severity of action. There has been increased publicity in recent years and consequently bullying seems to have become more open and "fun" (as termed by some) than private and endured.

There are few statistics charting the growth of bullying incidents, although some argue that it hasn't increased but has just become more reported in the media and thus heightened in people's awareness of it. However, it is worth noting that aspects of bullying are the commonest causes for phone calls to ChildLine. Over 22,000 such calls were made in 1999[8]. In Scotland there is even a special ChildLine Bullying Line. Unfortunately when the Government collects child abuse figures, bullying is not one of the categories covered.

What is "bullying"? Many young people experience more than one type, so the following percentages add up to more than 100%:
- 66% Name-calling and teasing
- 49% Physical attack
- 27% Verbal or written threats
- 9% Extortion
- 3% Racial harassment
- 3% Isolation ["being sent to Coventry"]
- 3% Sexual intimidation
- 23% Other types, or not recorded.[9]

In his book about bullying, Kevin Brown describes bullying essentially as the intention "to damage another person's self-esteem, thereby reducing the latter's sense of personal power and consequently the ability to pose a threat."[10] The Russian psychologist, Maslow, identified five basic human needs in his work at the beginning of the 20th century. The most basic was survival, then safety, then love, then self-esteem, and finally self-actualisation. So the loss of self-esteem through bullying is especially important as it affects a key part of an individual's personal needs.

A survey in 2000 by Scripture Union revealed that 29% of young people fear being bullied at school,[11] up from 25% in a large survey published in 1995.[12] So serious is the problem that in November 2001 a day conference was held at the Royal College of Physicians chaired by the Prime Minister's wife, Cherie Booth QC.[13] Bullying does not only take place at school unfortunately, and can also happen at home or outside school.

The RAKES Survey

The study asked three questions related to bullying, with the replies showing that 3% of the respondents thought they were a "bully", 17% said that over the previous three months they had intentionally tried to hurt someone physically, and 20% said they had intentionally tried to hurt someone's feelings. However, it did not ask respondents if they had ever been the subject of bullying.

The percentage saying they would describe themselves as a bully increased as their academic success decreased, as illustrated below.

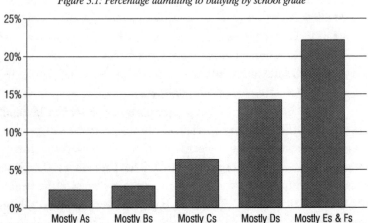

Figure 3.1: Percentage admitting to bullying by school grade

More than a fifth, 22%, of those who mostly got E and F grades would describe themselves as a bully against 2% of those who mostly got grade A. Is this behaviour outside the classroom in some way to compensate for what they lack in the classroom?

The overall percentage of 3% did not vary by age, gender or the frequency with which they went to church (if at all). It did vary, however, by Christian commitment – 2% who said they either were a Christian or weren't sure if they were admitted to being a bully, against 4% of those who were no longer a Christian, 7% who had never been a Christian and 10% who belonged to another religion.

Of the 17% who had intentionally tried to physically hurt some-one in the previous three months, two-thirds, 68%, were boys and one-third girls. The overall percentage did not vary by age or academic success, but did for churchgoing: for those who went regularly the percentage was 14%, for those who went occasionally 15%, for those who had stopped going 18% and for those who had never been 25%.

This shows that those who attend church with greater frequency are less likely to want to hurt someone physically (although at one in every 7, 14%, it may be thought it was still far too high!). This find-ing supports the thesis of Professor Robin Gill who affirms that the more frequently a person attends church the stronger their values.[14] The percentage also varied by religious commitment – 14% for those who were Christian, 21% for those who were not sure, 23% who were no longer a Christian, 26% for those who never were and 20% for those in another religion.

These results show that going to church regularly or being a Christian does make a difference to a person's behaviour, though neither made any difference to the proportion who had intentionally tried to hurt someone's feelings!

The experience of school

Asking "What do you like best about school?" in the Focus Groups produced a list of subjects they liked, some rather flippant answers such as "The end of it!", but also some replies that underline the preferences and values of this age-group:

"The place to interact with people"

"Somewhere to make friends"

"If you work hard you can get something good out of it at the end"

"Lunchtime, because you can eat and be with your friends"

"Lunchtime, because it's the longest break"

"All the sport"

Friends, food and fun (sport?) are important to this age-group and featured again and again.

What they liked least about school came down to two main factors: duties and teachers. Along with detentions and the amount of homework, they didn't like:

"Having to do rubbish duty"

"The way teachers tell you off"

"Teachers who don't let you have your say"

"Insane teachers", "Boring teachings", "Rubbish teachers"

"Teachers who teach you things you don't need to know"

"Teachers who talk too much and don't make it interesting"

"Teachers I don't understand" (said by several)

These responses imply that these Tweenagers have fairly clear ideas on how they want to learn and which teachers meet their expectations. It would have been interesting to ask the churchgoers whether those who teach them at church met the same standards they look for in their school teachers, or are some of them also considered insane, boring, or rubbish!

They were also asked which two subjects they would leave out of the school curriculum if they could. The purpose of this question was to see whether RE would be mentioned. It was, but only by one boy. Maths, sciences and foreign languages fared much worse! When asked why, their answers were a mix of not liking the teacher, thinking the teacher did not teach the subject well or finding the particular subject hard.

The Scottish Tweenagers were asked what they thought were the differences between what they were taught in RME (Religious and Moral Education, the equivalent of RE in England and Wales) and in church. Answers fell into two groups:

Item	RME	Church
Material taught	Deals with basic history Includes other religions	Looks also at meaning Only teaches Christianity
Teaching methods	It's compulsory – people are there unwillingly	It is voluntary
	"It feels more like work"	It can be fun
	All taught in the same way	Wider range of things to do

The Scottish youngsters were also asked how going to church helped them at school. Answers included:

"When in tight situations such as in sports, it teaches you how you should react"

"It helps you know what is morally right, so it helps in making decisions"

"Friends I know at school come to church, and some of them come to youth group with me."

Lord Dearing's Report

Much attention was focused on church schools, or "faith schools", in 2001 partly as the consequence of Lord Dearing's Report[15] suggesting that the Church of England set up or take over more than 100 comprehensive schools "over the next seven or eight years", a proposal widely supported by the General Synod in its November 2001 meeting, and apparently, by the Government, too. This is "a challenge we dare not miss", wrote Bishop Michael Marshall, as the report "could well prove to be of strategic importance in the turnaround of the missionary enterprise of our Church."[16]

Lord Dearing quotes the Archbishop of Canterbury:

"Education is about forming people who have the moral strength and spiritual depth to hold to a course and weather its ups and downs.

It is about forming people who know that economic competition is not more important than family life and love of neighbour, and that technical innovation is not more important than reverence for the beauty of creation. It is about forming people who, however academically and technically skilful, are not reduced to inarticulate embarrassment by the great questions of life and death, meaning and truth.

Church Schools embody the truth that a context of firm principles suffused by faith and love is the best and right basis for learning and growing."[17]

Church Schools

In 2000 the Church of England was responsible for 4,500 primary schools, a quarter of the country's total, and the Roman Catholics 1,800 or a tenth. Thus over a third of primary schools are Church Schools. The Church of England is responsible for far fewer secondary schools – about 200 or 3% of the total – although the Catholics are responsible for 9%, three times as many.

The impact of Church Schools, Anglican and Catholic, has been much researched by Professor Leslie Francis.[18] In general he finds young people attending these schools positive about them, especially if their parents are either practising churchgoers, or never attend church. Young people's attitudes to such schools and Religious Education (RE) are more likely to be negative, however, if their parents are only nominally Christian.[19] Similar findings have been found in parallel studies in Australia.[20, 21] The values these schools espouse are very important to pupils[22] (as well as to their parents).

Entrance requirements to Church Schools vary. Some schools are very strict: in over-subscribed Catholic schools in London, head teachers "ask not only whether prospective pupils go to church, but whether they play an active role in the parish and whether their parents subscribe to Catholic teaching."[23]

Some are less strict but potential pupils' parents must be regular churchgoers, resulting in some parents joining a church for this purpose, estimated, however, at only 2% in a 2001 study.[24] Other schools allocate a percentage of places to children of non-churchgoing parents.

Church Schools are increasingly popular with parents who see them as promoting more upright moral behaviour as well as teaching religious beliefs. While it may be the former more than the latter that attracts parents, this popularity is an affirmation of what parents desire for their children. However, this assumes that Church Schools retain their distinctive religious ethos. Some today feel that they don't, especially in RE lessons, and that some teachers in Church Schools are not supportive of Christian values.

There are a number of independent schools with a strong Christian ethos, most of which were founded in the 19th century. Many of these encourage and expect regular church attendance, often at the school chapel.

A number of new independent Christian schools were established in the 1990s, almost all evangelical, partly because of the way certain subjects are often taught (for example, evolution) and partly because parents desired a stronger discipline. These retain a very lively and distinctive Christian ethos, and are generally found to be enthusiastically endorsed by pupils and parents alike. In a study of one Pentecostal church in Essex which had a school attached to the church, 27% of those attending the church said one of the things they most valued was the school.[25]

Both in the UK and the United States[26] these newer schools are seen as helping forward the mission of the church not only by teaching Christianity but also teaching pupils to live a Christian life and to share their faith with others. A real involvement with the community is warmly encouraged.

One recent study by Professor Leslie Francis on Catholic schools in Scotland[27], has shown that Catholic students educated in Catholic schools hold a more positive attitude towards Christianity than Catholic students educated in non-Catholic schools. On the other hand, non-Catholic students in Catholic schools held a less positive attitude!

Many schools, church and otherwise, welcome the involvement of external specialists for RE or other lessons and school assemblies. Youth for Christ is one organisation undertaking such tasks, and, by all reports, doing it very effectively. 75% of their contacts are through schools, with RE lessons and assemblies allowing them to meet 1,100 children per week on average[28].

Parents and Schools

The parental role changed over the last few decades of the 20th century. Before 1980 school life was "the secret garden of learning" often separated from home life. Parents were passive recipients of the school's views about their children. There was a "professional-isation" of learning, and teachers took the attitude that "this is our job – we know how to teach your children."

During the 1980s and 1990s this changed as parents were given greater freedom to choose the schools they wanted for their children. They were seen as consumers and purchasers of education, who could attend annual meetings and ask sometimes awkward questions. Schools learned to become more accountable to parents.

In the 21st century there are more parents on governing bodies, and parent governors can join Local Education Authority education committees. As a consequence parents have a greater say in how schools are run, and they are seen as having a crucial role in their children's education. Thousands assist in classrooms daily. Home-school agreements were launched in September 1999, and teachers now have a professional obligation to consult with parents of pupils.[29]

The challenge thus is for Christian parents to consider how to choose an appropriate school, be involved, establish a good working relationship with the school and support it as practically as possible. It also means helping them to think biblically about education – and discipline.[30]

The challenge also for the church is to know how best to help parents with their educational responsibilities. Nowhere is this more important than in the transition from junior to secondary school. One church in south London has a meeting every August for children moving up from junior school "to help them think Christianly" when they enter a new world where many of their previous friends are no longer present. Youth for Christ also regularly work with the top two years of junior schools and then meet again with the children in their secondary schools as a point of continuity to make the transition easier and for there to be a familiar friend throughout.

One help is *our schools magazine* (OSM), available in 18 English counties and in South Wales, with 630,000 copies of each issue distributed free. It aims "to inform teachers, families and children of current events, courses, attractions etc." and will include relevant religious items as appropriate.[31] Scripture Union's material to aid this transition is *It's your Move*.

What then is the influence of the school on young people? Huge! And not least in spiritual matters, as we shall see. But the influence is one which in many instances churches can help shape. "Schools are doorways to their local community"[32] and involvement with schools gives churches the opportunity to touch many more than just their pupils. So school involvement is vital, and one reason why 78% of Youth For Christ[33], Scripture Union and the Schools Ministry Network workers, for example, are committed to such.

Services in schools

In December 2001 Bishop Michael Nazir-Ali met clergy and others in Dartford Deanery, in his Anglican Diocese of Rochester. He suggested holding services in school halls after school had finished.

One of those present, Rev Francis Willoughby, Vicar of Sutton-at-Hone decided he would try it. He wrote to parents suggesting that a short service on a weekday, after school finished, might be a solution to the problem of getting to Sunday worship at the local church. The only reply he got was from someone who couldn't come but wished him well!

So they put out twenty chairs on the day, prepared songs familiar to the children, and waited. By 3.10 pm 55 parents had arrived, and by the time the service was under way the caretaker was out searching for more chairs for the assembled "congregation". It lasted 20 minutes, and such was the positive response that a similar service will now be held twice a term. Francis Willoughby subsequently wrote to the neighbouring Horton Kirby School to hold services there too![34]

So where does all this take us?

This brief chapter has shown:
- School is a very important part of the Tweenagers' world.
- They have clear ideas on what they like and dislike about school. They like meeting friends, eating, having fun and sport. They dislike subjects they find hard and teachers who do not get their subject across well. However, RE is not singled out as a subject they would choose to drop.
- A "comfortable school" includes opportunities for quietness. Could nearby churches provide this?
- A "safe school" is one free from bullying, which almost a third of children fear. Bullying damages a Tweenager's self-esteem.
- In the RAKES survey 3% of respondents, more than 60 children, admitted to being a "bully". But for those whose academic success was limited to mostly getting Grades E and F the percentage rose to 22%.

- In the survey also, one in six, 17%, admitted to trying intentionally to hurt someone physically in the previous three months, twice as many boys as girls. This was a little less for those with higher expectations of academic success or those who said they were Christian.
- A fifth, 20%, also admitted to trying intentionally to hurt someone's feelings in the previous three months, which did not vary by age, gender, academic level or faith.
- Church schools provide an important opportunity to reflect and teach the morals and beliefs of Christianity. Their popularity indicates many parents wish to affirm such values.
- Parents have many more opportunities now to influence how schools are run. Can churches encourage greater participation?
- Schools are doorways to the local community, allowing special opportunities for churches with school links.

NOTES

[1] Socrates 425–399 BC. Quoted from *Pray4Change,* issued by Crusaders, Issue One, Winter 2000, Page 2.

[2] *Essential Youth,* Rev Andy Hickford, Kingsway, 1998, Page 125.

[3] *Education, The Guardian,* 5 June 2001.

[4] Ibid., Page 3.

[5] Ibid., Page 3.

[6] *Outcomes in Secondary Education for children excluded in Primary School,* Research Brief from Department for Employment and Education, No. 271, May 2001, Page 1.

[7] *The Brat Pack,* 11–14 year olds – how do you treat yours?, John and Sue Ritter, Marshall Pickering, HarperCollinsReligious, London, 1994, Page 115.

[8] *ChildLine has now helped more than one million children,* Leaflet, 1999.

[9] Ibid.

[10] *Bullying, What can Parents Do?,* Kevin Brown, Monarch, Crowborough, 1997, Page 29.

[11] Report by Claire Shelley in the *Church of England Newspaper,* 8 December 2000.

[12] *Fast-moving currents in Youth Culture,* edited by Leslie Francis, William Kay, Alan Kerbey and Olaf Fogwill, Lynx Communications, Oxford, 1995.

[13] *NewsLine,* News for ChildLine supporters, Autumn 2001.

[14] *Churchgoing and Christian Ethics,* Professor Robin Gill, CUP, 1999.

[15] *The Way Ahead: Church of England Schools in the New Millennium,* Lord Dearing, Archbishops' Council, 2001.

[16] Article in the *Church of England Newspaper,* 22 June 2001, Page 7.

[17] Op cit., Item 15, taken from article "What makes a Christian school?" by Michael Hepworth in *The Daily Telegraph,* 31 July, 2002, Page 15.

[18] See, for example, the research from various studies summarised in Chapter 5 of *Reaching and Keeping Teenagers,* Peter Brierley, MARC, Tunbridge Wells, 1993, or in *Youth Spirituality* detailed below.

[19] As, for example, the research described in *Religious Trends* No 1, 1998/1999, edited by Peter Brierley, Christian Research, London and Paternoster Publishing, Carlisle, 1997, Page 5.3.

[20] *Youth Spirituality,* A summary of published research relating to youth spirituality, religiosity and values, Rev Dr Philip Hughes and Sharon Bond, Christian Research Association for Uniting Education, Melbourne, 2001.

[21] Articles by Rev Dr Philip Hughes in *Pointers,* Christian Research Association Bulletin, Sydney, Australia, such as in Volume 9, Number 3, Page 12, September 1999.

[22] Article "Integrating Faith and Learning: an empirical case study from a Church of England Secondary School" by Ruth Deakin Crick in *Whitefield Briefing,* Volume 7, Number 1, March 2002.

[23] Article by Annabel Miller in *The Tablet,* 12 May 2001, Page 689.

[24] *Faith in Life,* Churches Information for Mission, Alison Gelder and Dr Phillip Escott, 2001.

[25] Research report for Peniel Pentecostal Church, Congregational Attitudes and Beliefs Survey, Christian Research, London, November 2001, Page 12.

[26] See, for example, article by Paul Mueller "Christian Day Schools Missionary Outposts" in *Strategies for Today's Leader,* Corunna, Indiana, United States, Summer 2000, Page 18.

[27] Article "Growing up Catholic in a Scottish City: The relationship between denominational identity, denominational schools, and attitude towards Christianity among 11–15 year olds" in *Catholic Education: A Journal of Inquiry and Practice,* Volume 5, Number 1, September 2001, Page 39.

[28] *Quadrant,* special edition, 2002, Christian Research and Youth For Christ, PO Box 5254, Halesowen, Birmingham B63 3DG.

[29] Taken from an article "Parents and Schools in Partnership" in *Breakthrough,* the magazine from CARE, London, Summer 2001, Page 12.

[30] See, for example, the paper *Loving is Not Smacking,* Calling the Church to speak out to end the physical punishment of Children, by Christine Dodd, Popanva, Derbyshire, 1999. A group of Christian schools challenged in court in 2001 the rulings against corporal punishment.

[31] Details of OSM Publications are available through their Head Office on 0118 940 2060.

[32] Op cit., Andy Hickford, Page 155.

[33] *FactFile,* Audit of Contacts in 1997, Christian Research and Youth For Christ, No 5, Summer 1998, Page 1 and 75% in 2001 (Footnote 28).

[34] Reported in the *Rochester LINK,* March 2002.

The importance of the small screen

With over 99% of households in Britain having a television, there are virtually no young people today who grow up without being able to watch one, and in the few homes without there will often be the opportunity to watch some programmes at school.

This chapter looks primarily at the importance of television and the world beyond it through the internet; other aspects of the media come in the next chapter.

Watching Television

This survey confirmed that watching television was the most popular activity of Tweenagers in their spare time; only 2% did not watch it. Half, 50%, reckoned on watching it by themselves, a quarter, 27%, with friends, and a fifth, 21%, with others. The percentages were consistent across the age range and for both young men and women.

What did they watch? Four types of programme were watched by a majority; they were:
- 81% Comedy
- 79% Films
- 67% Soaps
- 58% Cartoons

These answers are consistent with BBC Research which shows that the most popular programmes watched by young people aged 13 to 15 in 1999 were EastEnders, the Vicar of Dibley, the film Mission Impossible, and Coronation Street (followed by Who wants to be a Millionaire? and Walking with Dinosaurs)[1].

For the Focus Group youngsters The Simpsons was by far the most watched programme (11 of the 17), followed by EastEnders (8), Neighbours (2) and Friends (1). No other specific programme was named, but 6 of them (all boys!) watch football. They were asked why they watched these programmes, and 'fun' was mentioned again and again. Other replies were to do with relaxing, something to do when they are bored, to be "cheered up", and "to keep up to date for school" – which was not to do with school work but about knowing what was happening in the programmes so they could talk about it knowledgeably with their friends.

One of the reasons why Tweenagers don't like church is because it is not "fun". If their understanding of "fun" is these types of programmes, then the gap between them and average church activities is very wide.

What other kinds of programme did they watch? Minorities watched:

- 47% Sport/leisure
- 44% Game shows
- 37% Quiz shows
- 25% News
- 24% Animals/nature
- 23% DIY/gardening
- 20% Documentaries

Smaller percentages still watched Cookery (14%), Information (9%), Current affairs (7%), Religious (7%), and Discussion programmes (6%). While it may be encouraging that 7% of Tweenagers watch religious programmes, 36% of this sample said they went to church regularly, and 55% said they were Christian, so the popularity of religious TV with this age-group is not huge even among the committed (but this may simply reflect that suitable programmes are not there to be watched!).

The popularity of some of these programmes varied with gender as Figure 4.1 indicates; the remainder did not vary between young men and women.

Likewise some programmes were more popular with younger Tweenagers than with older. If we take younger Tweenagers as aged 11 or under and older ones as 12 or over, then the programmes which varied significantly by age are those shown in Figure 4.2.

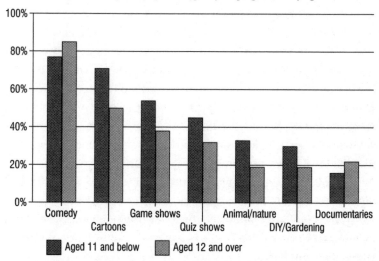

Figure 4.1: Popularity of four types of TV programmes by gender

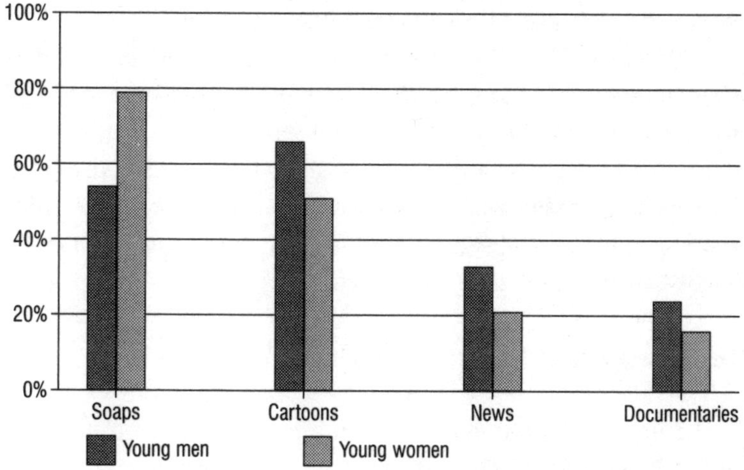

Figure 4.2: Popularity of seven types of TV programmes by age

Older Tweenagers prefer comedy and documentaries, and younger Tweenagers the other types shown. The biggest difference is between gender on the soaps and between age on the cartoons.

There is a huge interest in the impact of television on young people, and much research has been devoted to this end, especially looking at the impact of violence. A whole issue of *Communication Research Trends* was devoted to the topic[2].

Professor Leslie Francis has also researched television viewing[3]. He confirms that what is watched varies with age and gender, and also by social class. He also found that total *time* spent watching TV depended on the programmes available, in other words if there was nothing on that young people wished to watch they wouldn't watch just anything as a substitute. They picked certain programmes of interest and watched those, rather than watching whatever came on.

Television and churchgoing

Leslie Francis has found that church attendance is correlated with both the amount of TV and the types of programmes which are watched. Thus churchgoers generally watch less TV than non-goers, but watch "more current awareness programmes" for example[4].

How far was this true in the RAKES survey? The answers support Leslie Francis' work in an interesting way. Whether a Tweenager was a Christian, or thought they were, or knew they weren't did not make any difference to programmes watched, except for religious programmes. But when analysed by whether or not a Tweenager went to church regularly, it did. Leslie Francis did not look at how television viewing varied by belief systems but by church attendance, and the RAKES survey also found this difference significant.

Table 4.3 details the types of programme where this difference shows and reveals that regular Tweenager churchgoers are more likely to watch news, animal/nature, DIY/gardening and religious programmes and less likely to watch comedy, films, soaps, sport and discussion programmes than non-regulars. It is interesting that all the programmes watched more by Tweenagers are factual, and most of those watched less are not.

Table 4.3: Church attendance by type of programme watched on television

Type of programme	Regular %	Occasional %	Lapsed %	Never %	*Overall* %
Comedy	77	84	84	87	82
Films	75	82	81	83	79
Soaps	62	68	73	71	68
Sport/leisure	40	51	47	55	47
News	29	26	23	22	26
Animal/nature	28	26	24	19	25
DIY/gardening	27	24	21	19	23
Cookery	16	16	15	10	14
Religious	12	4	5	3	7
Discussion	5	7	9	5	6

Cartoons (very popular for nearly all this age-group), current affairs, documentaries, game shows, information and quiz shows were watched equally by regular churchgoers and non-goers.

Equipment owned

Tweenagers today own a lot of personal equipment. The following percentages said they personally owned:
- 80% Music system
- 74% Computer
- 66% Personal stereo
- 62% Mobile phone
- 61% Personal CD
- 61% Playstation or Dreamcast or N64
- 35% Televideo
- 22% DVD
- 10% WAP phone
- 4% Playnet

In addition 61% had a TV and 36% a video player in their room. The first percentage is slightly higher than the 52% of under-16s with a TV in their room as measured by Independent Television[5], but this may be because this study focuses only on Tweenagers rather than all those under 16. The percentages are in any case very comparable.

Similar percentages of Tweenagers in the Focus Groups owned such equipment, but an attempt was made to find out the relative values of these by asking the question, "If your house was on fire and you just had time to choose one of them to rescue, which would it be?" There was a definite gender preference in both groups: boys were more likely to take the TV or the play station, while the girls would definitely prefer their mobile phone.

Personal access to music, computer, mobile and television are crucial for Tweenagers in the 21st century. It is around these that their world revolves, and therefore a key source for their understanding of the world and its values. While television is important, it does actually come fourth on this list, and comes after music and computer (which in this context is virtually synonymous with "internet").

The percentages accessing music and a computer were the same for both genders, but girls were more likely than boys to have a mobile phone (67% to 58%) and boys more than girls to have a TV in their room (66% to 57%). However boys were twice as likely to have a WAP phone (14% to 7%). Girls owned more CD players (65% to 56%), but boys were much more likely to have a PlayStation (79% to 48%). Boys want challenge and technology; girls friends and music.

Ownership of some of these items varied with age as shown in Figure 4.4. It seems that when a young person enters secondary school or the year after they are bought equipment which presumably many others in their classes have.

According to a *Daily Mail* survey about the same time as RAKES 90% of British children owned a mobile phone, much higher than the 62% reported above[6]. They also found that 10% of these used their phone for 45 minutes a day.

Figure 4.4: Personal ownership of equipment by age

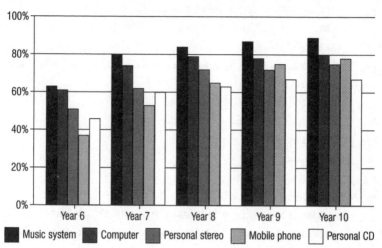

The largest difference is in the ownership of a mobile phone but the rapid growth of ownership shown in this diagram may but reflect the huge overall explosion of ownership of such phones, especially by young people in the years 1999 and 2000. This probably explains the difference in the Target Group Index survey in 2000 which found 49% of 11–14 year olds with a mobile phone[7], and commented "their funds are now channelled into CDs and phone vouchers."

It might be wondered how young people of this age can afford such items? Presumably the equipment itself is given to them as gifts. The cost of keeping it working is reflected in the fact that the average pocket money of 11 to 16 year olds was under £5 per week in 2000, but just under £7 in 2001![8] Girls have more pocket money than boys[9].

Internet access

Internet access is also almost universal:
- Four-fifths, 81%, and all but one in the Focus Groups, had access both to a computer and to the internet[10];
- One-eighth, 13%, had access to a computer but not the internet;
- Leaving just 6% with no access to a computer and hence not the internet.

How often did this 81% access the internet?
- 11% accessed it more than once a day
- 30% once a day
- 37% once a week
- 11% once a month,
- 11% less than once a month.

If these frequencies are treated respectively as 500 times a year, 365 times, 52 times, 12 times and 5 times, then the average number of times that those with access to the internet went online was 186 times a year. This varied by age:
- 10 years: 163 times a year
- 11 years: 166
- 12 years: 199
- 13 years: 203
- 14 years: 224 times a year.

Those accustomed to most academic success (normally getting A grades) were rather more likely to have access to a computer than those getting E or F grades (98% to 89%).

In comparison with American teenagers these Tweenagers are using the internet a lot! 89% of the 81% of Tweenagers with access do so at least once a month, that is 72% of all Tweenagers. That compares with 41% of Americans in this age-group in August 1999[11], and although in the two years gap the American percentage probably increased, it is unlikely to have gone as high as the Brits! Perhaps the American dominance in email traffic is lessening.

The RAKES study did not ask whether the internet access was at home or at school (or elsewhere), but other studies put access in this age-group at 43% having home access in 2000[12] (which varied between 62% in social classes A and B, 45% for C1 and C2, and 24% for those in D or E). Even allowing for the year's difference between the two studies the gap is very large, suggesting that perhaps almost half of internet access is at school.

It is affected by whether they have their own bedroom. As we have already seen, five-sixths, 84%, of the young people in this study had a room to themselves. Of these virtually all, 96%, had access to a computer (against 90% with such access who shared a room).

Basic internet use

What is the internet used for? Seven suggestions were made on the form with an open option. The replies were:
- 67% E-mails
- 67% Information
- 55% Play games
- 41% Play music
- 33% Chat rooms
- 16% Shopping
- 10% News
- 17% Other uses.

Correspondence, facts – presumably for help with school work – and fun are the three prime uses of the internet for Tweenagers. These results are almost identical with those of another survey on why teenagers go online[13].

Gender variations: Girls used the internet for e-mails more than boys (72% to 62%), a similar difference to that of mobile phone ownership, which underlines that making or keeping in touch with friends is more important to girls. Boys used it more for playing games (64% to 47%) and for news (14% to 6%). But for other uses, the genders were on a par.

Age variations: Older Tweenagers (aged 12 and over) used the internet for e-mail more than younger ones (11 and below) by 71% to 61%, and twice as much for the chat rooms (41% to 21%). However, younger ones used it for playing games more those older (63% to 50%). For other uses, age made no difference.

School grade variations: Variations in use for different levels of school grade are shown in Figure 4.5. Other uses had no such variations, but these indicate that the higher the grades a Tweenager was accustomed to get the more they would use the internet to get information, and the less they would use it as a chat room. Presumably they take their school work more seriously or are assigned homework which is helped by internet use. The use of the internet for e-mail was more ambivalent, and varied less.

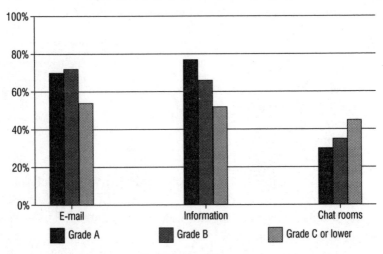

Figure 4.5: Use of the internet by academic grade

Frequency of use variations: The frequency with which the internet was used varied by the purpose for which it was being used. Thus while 67% of Tweenagers said they used the internet for e-mails such use averaged 219 times a year. Likewise 67% of Tweenagers may have obtained information or news from the internet at some time, but these were the least often used features.

This compares with those who use it for chat rooms (250 times a year on average), playing music (240 times a year), using the shopping facilities (228 times a year), playing games (211 times a year) and other uses (on average, 206 times a year).

Church attendance variations: Did those who went to church use the internet more or less than those who did not? This is illustrated in Figure 4.6.

Regular churchgoers tend to use the internet more for information than others, and use it less for playing games or music, or for chat rooms or for shopping. Apart from chat room use, there is little difference between occasional churchgoers and those who no longer go. And for information, games or music, those who never go to church are noticeably different from the rest.

Figure 4.6: Use of the internet by frequency of church attendance

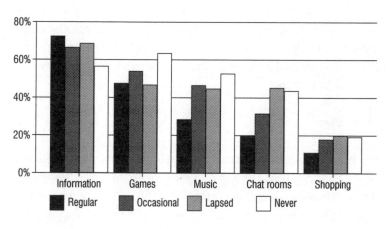

How they value the internet

As with other factors, the Focus Groups gave the opportunity to explore some of these issues in more depth. The Tweenagers were asked what they thought was good and bad about the internet.

Good things about the internet:
- The variety of sites, especially ones helpful for school work: "You can find out loads of things" and "You can get good information for school".
- The possibilities it offers: games to download, TV pro-gramme websites, etc.
- The contacts it makes possible: chat lines, email and live web links enabling them to talk to people.

Bad about things about it:
- The technical aspects: "It takes ages to download", "It crashes too often", "It takes ages to log on", "There are too many things with passwords".
- The cost: sites which have to be paid for combined with fam-ily disagreements about who pays for their internet usage!
- The content: too many adverts, junk emails, "stupid stuff", and "too much that you don't need".

These Tweenagers were most interested in the internet for the relationships it offers, the possibilities to have fun, and the help it can give in school work. However, they are reasonably discerning about the downsides of the internet, apparently more so than they are with television.

Other internet use

A sixth of the respondents said they used the internet for "other pur-poses", but only just over half of these actually said what they did use it for. The most popular other use – about a third of those giving an "other" or 3% of the total – was "homework". Others amplified this as "research for homework" or "revision" or "schoolwork".

The next most common use, 1.3%, was surfing or browsing, or searching websites[14]. Then came, at 1.0%, obtaining mobile phone logos or texts or ringing tones. Writing and obtaining messages through the MSN messenger service was mentioned by 14 Tweenagers. Sending text messages developed into a particular

Tweenager craze (if the daily newspapers are to be believed) in the autumn of 2001. It also has its Christian advocates, such as the following version of Psalm 23 (whose 258 characters fit into two messages)[15]:

> "Wiv da Lord watchin ova me, I av evryfin I need. He calms my storms+lets me rst peacfuly. He gives me strenth+leads me down da rite paths 4 my own gd. Evn in a midnite alley, bcoz of da Lord im nt afraid – im comfortd by him. He keeps on givin 2 me no mattr wot. Gods gdness+luv wil be wiv me always_il liv wiv da Lord 4eva."

Then came porn, also at 0.6%, which may seem very small, but is almost certainly larger than this as many would be frightened of mentioning it. That some young people use the internet for this, however, is confirmed from other studies. One showed that children as young as 10 years were using it[16]. Up to a fifth of children under 17 visited such sites at least once a month, watching it for 28 minutes on average. 8% of the children watching porn are 10 or under, which means that the other 92% are aged 11 to 16. So it is very likely that the small percentage in this study is only the tip of an iceberg.

Other uses included games, sport, cheats (for electronic games), and specific sites in which a Tweenager had a particular interest. The type of use that emerges from the above supports the comment "people, not products, drive the internet"[17]. In case the above findings suggest otherwise, there are sites which offer "good, clean fun for kids"[18].

Can the internet be used to reach out in a spiritual way to young people? YES, would argue Richard Bromley of Youth for Christ, who has already experimented with doing so, and found that it works. They also have a SMS texting ministry, using it to link with a variety of young people, extending the length and depth of contact to form more significant relationships which then encourages the young people to visit their web page and chat room. The key features of their internet ministry are[19]:

- To demonstrate to young people the faith of those using the internet by what they do and how they have lived their lives
- To be always available when they need help
- To ensure that it is safe for them to talk about anything
- To act as a friend, there for them.

So what does this all add up to?

This chapter has shown:
- Virtually every teenager watched television in their spare time. The most popular programmes were comedy, films, soaps and cartoons.
- Soaps were more popular with young women, the others with young men.
- Comedy and documentaries were more popular with older Tweenagers, cartoons, game and quiz shows, animal/nature and DIY with younger Tweenagers.
- Regular Tweenager churchgoers were more likely to watch news, animal/nature, DIY/gardening and religious programmes than non-regulars, and less likely to watch comedy, films, soaps, sport and discussion programmes.
- Tweenagers only watched television when the content was of interest to them. They did not watch it for general relaxation. Presumably therefore they only like church when the content is of interest to them.
- Three out of four Tweenagers had their own music system and computer. Two-thirds had a personal stereo, mobile phone, personal CD, playstation and a TV in their room. Girls were more likely to have a mobile phone, boys a TV in their room. Ownership of all these increased with age, especially after a year or so at secondary school.
- Much of Tweenage pocket money is spent on music and mobile phones.

- Four-fifths of Tweenagers had access to the internet. Of these, over three-quarters accessed it at least once a week, and almost half at least once a day. One in nine accessed it several times a day. [Averaged over all Tweenagers, these percentages are respectively 63% weekly, 33% daily, and 9% more often].
- Those likely to get greater academic success accessed the internet more than others, and more often to acquire information.
- The main uses of the internet were for emails, information and to play games. There was a wide range of more minor usage, including a small percentage who admitted using it for porn. Tweenagers appear to be more discriminating about their use of the internet than they are of what they watch on television.
- Usage varied by age, gender and academic success. Also different purposes were used at different frequencies – so email was used by many frequently, information was used by many but much less frequently, chat rooms were used by a few but very frequently, and so on.
- Friendship is more important to girls, with more of them owning a mobile phone, and more use of emails by them.
- Regular churchgoers used the internet less for most purposes, but more for information.

All this adds up to a huge influence on Tweenagers of television, music, mobile phones and computers/internet. They select from TV, music and internet information that other people have produced, but they create for themselves the text messages they send via mobiles or when they interchange via email or across a chat room. There is also a substantial proportion of "fun" in their use of this technology, whether games on the internet or a PlayStation. Churches need to provide suitable content, allow creativity, in a context of fun if they are to attract this generation.

NOTES

[1] *Social Focus on Young People,* National Statistics, The Stationery Office, 2000, Table 5.4.

[2] *Communication Research Trends,* Centre for the Study of Communication and Culture, Saint Louis University, Athens, Ohio, United States, Volume 19, Numbers 1 and 2, 1999.

[3] For example, "The influence of age, sex and social class on TV Viewing Time and Programme preferences among 11–15 year olds", Professor Leslie Francis and Harry Gibson, in the *Journal of Educational Television,* Volume 19, Number 1, 1993.

[4] Ibid.

[5] *The Burden of Youth,* Opportunities and Aspirations, a reported commissioned from the Henley Centre by the Salvation Army, 2001, Page 15, figure for 2001.

[6] Source of information: Footnote on Page 43 of *Christianity+Renewal,* September 2001.

[7] Ibid.

[8] Ibid., quoting the Walls' Pocket Money Monitor.

[9] Article in *The Face,* No 66, July 2002, Page 69.

[10] Perhaps through their school.

[11] Internet interest, in *Wired,* www.navpress.com, January 2000.

[12] Ibid., quoting the Target Group Index for 2000.

[13] Detailed in a comprehensive summary report *The use of the Internet for Evangelism,* Richard Bromley, Youth for Christ, 2001.

[14] Web-surfing is a pastime of 70% of US teenagers, according to *Current Thoughts and Trends,* www.navpress.com, May 2001.

[15] Quoted in the *Church of England Newspaper,* 10 August 2001, and to be published in *Txt msgs from God,* Scripture Union, 2002.

[16] Report in the *Daily Telegraph,* 10 May 2001, from a study by NetValue, an Internet monitoring firm.

[17] *Current Thoughts and Trends,* www.navpress.com, July 2000.

[18] Such as www.cyberkids.com, recommended in *Time* magazine, 4 June 2001, but there are many others also. See, for example, *God on the Net,* Vernon Blackmore, Marshall Pickering, 1999.

[19] Op cit., *The Use of the Internet for Evangelism.*

Friends and leisure activities

All Tweenagers have lots of time to do their own thing! Details of the key leisure activities of television and the internet were considered in the last chapter; this one looks at what else they do.

Spare time activities

There was one comprehensive question seeking to cover the majority of Tweenagers' spare time, and the answers to what they did and who with are given in the Table on the next page.

It shows that spare-time activities fall into four groups: those undertaken by virtually all Tweenagers (TV, listening to music, homework, hanging around, watching videos, cinemas and playing computer games), those undertaken by about five-sixths of Tweenagers (playing sport, reading books, rollerblading and other hobbies), those undertaken by half to two-thirds (going to discos, playing arcade games or going to a youth club), and those undertaken by a minority (church activities and boy/girl friending). The same kind of mixture applied to those in the Focus Groups, with TV and hanging around with friends the clear favourites. However, one other activity was very popular which was not asked on the questionnaire – shopping! This was most popular for the girls but was also mentioned by a couple of the boys.

Top solitary occupations are doing homework, reading books and comics and listening to music. Top spare time activities with friends are simply hanging around with them, going to the cinema, discos/nightclubs or playing sports. Peer support is very important

Table 5.1: Tweenagers' spare time activities and companions

			I do it:		
Activity	TOTAL %	...on my own %	...with friends %	...with others %	I don't do it %
Watch television	98	50	27	21	2
Listen to music	97	67	26	4	3
Do homework	95	84	6	5	5
Hang around with friends	95	4	88	3	5
Watch videos/DVDs	94	25	52	17	6
Go to the cinema	94	2	77	15	6
Play computer/video games	91	59	25	7	9
Play team sports	83	3	57	23	17
Read books and comics	82	77	4	1	18
Other hobbies/interests	82	23	45	14	18
Skate/rollerblade/cycle	82	21	52	9	18
Discos/night clubs	68	1	60	7	32
Play arcade games	55	13	36	6	45
Youth/church club	52	4	39	9	48
Church activities	49	4	28	17	51
Hang out with boy-/girlfriend	46	25	19	2	54

for this age-group. Tweenagers might play sport with other people, watch television or videos/DVDs or attend church activities (but they may attend as a group together). It is interesting that despite the impression sometimes given in the media only half of this age-group spend time with a boy/girl friend, slightly less than were involved in church activities.

The next top solitary occupations are playing computer games and watching TV. But at the bottom of the solitary list are discos/nightclubs, youth clubs and church activities. That church activities should be in this final category shows the importance of attracting Tweenagers as a group rather than individually. The importance of the gang, apparent for older teenagers[1], is also true at this age.

Other activities

More than four-fifths in Table 5.1 answered that they had "other hobbies/ interests", and over three-quarters of these, 78%, indicated one or more of such other activities. The variety was huge! Table 5.2 gives a breakdown between indoor and outdoor activities, and the percentage of the total sample (not just this 78%) which did each one. A few of these replicated the main listing but not in such large numbers as to change the broad order of Table 5.1. The full detail of what activities are covered by each description is given in Appendix 4, Table A4/7.

Table 5.2: Other activities by broad location

Indoors	Number	% of total	Outdoors	Number	% of total
Swimming	122	5.6	Sport: Other	168	7.7
Musical instruments	120	5.5	Horse riding	65	3.0
Dancing	94	4.3	Shopping	51	2.3
Acting/drama	42	1.9	Cars and motorbikes	48	2.2
Inside hobbies	32	1.5	Sport: Football	46	2.1
Games	29	1.3	Youth organisations	39	1.8
Art and crafts	27	1.2	Sport: Tennis	26	1.2
Music: choir/singing	26	1.2	Athletics/gymnastics	25	1.2
Model making	25	1.2	Outside hobbies	25	1.2
Relationships	21	1.0	Skate/snow boarding	19	0.9
Collecting things	15	0.7	Animals	17	0.8
Ballet	12	0.6	Cycling	13	0.6
Spiritual	4	0.2			
TOTAL	569	26.2	TOTAL	542	25.0

Table 5.2 is important as it shows several things:

- The balance is virtually even between indoor and outdoor activities. Is this the average balance in youth club events?
- The main listing did not give swimming or playing music as options and it should have done. These two dominated the indoor activity. Youth clubs need to take their young people swimming – they love it! And if musical instruments are so important, with so many learning one, over a wide range, can churches use this interest, say with youth orchestras?
- Although the main list included "team sports", not every Tweenager thought of their sport in this way. Those who play sport take it seriously, though, and being part of a church football team, for example, can be crucial to developing faith.
- The list did not include dancing and should have done. Both sport and dancing are high energy! Both can be competitive. Can church youth clubs use such energy in a creative way?
- Nor did the list include horse-riding. It was not realised from the pilot study how popular this was: 3% of Tweenagers do this.

Variations by gender

Of the 16 activities listed in Table 5.1, eight varied by gender in the extent to which they were undertaken and/or with whom they did it, as Table 5.3 indicates.

Table 5.3 shows not just that some activities appeal more to males than females, but that in some, such as watching videos/DVDs or playing arcade games, males are much more likely to do them alone rather than with friends or others.

Female Tweenagers are more likely than males to hang around with friends, and with these friends to watch videos/DVDs, go to the cinema, discos/night clubs or church activities. Females go to church more anyway. Males play team sports or arcade games more with friends than do females, but females actually play arcade games (and home computer games) less.

The Table is helpful in deciding what activities a Tweenage youth club might undertake, and what would appeal most to whom.

Table 5.3: Tweenager spare time activity by gender

Activity		TOTAL %	I do it: ...on my own %	I do it: ...with friends %	I do it: ...with others %	I don't do it %
Hang around with friends	M	93	5	84	4	7
	F	97	2	92	3	3
Watch videos/DVDs	M	94	29	49	16	6
	F	94	20	57	17	6
Go to the cinema	M	93	3	73	17	7
	F	96	1	81	14	4
Play computer/video games	M	96	56	34	6	4
	F	87	62	18	7	13
Play team sports	M	87	4	64	19	13
	F	80	1	52	27	20
Discos/night clubs	M	60	2	50	8	40
	F	74	1	67	6	26
Play arcade games	M	72	20	47	5	28
	F	41	6	27	8	59
Church activities	M	43	4	23	16	57
	F	54	3	33	18	46

Variations by age

Likewise most types of Tweenage activity varied with age or school year, but watching TV, playing home computer or arcade games didn't. Table 5.4 shows the importance of young people doing things with friends. There is a clear increase in the middle column "with friends" from up to 11 years of age and over 11 for listening to music, hanging around with friends, watching videos, going to the cinema (an especially large increase), discos and night clubs, youth or church clubs, and spending time with a boy or girl friend.

The only two solitary activities which increased with age were homework and spending time with a boy/girl friend.

Table 5.4: Tweenager spare time activity by school years

			I do it:			
(<11: 11 or under; >11: 12 or over)	Age	TOTAL %	...on my own %	...with friends %	...with others %	I don't do it %
Listen to music	<11	96	69	22	5	4
	>11	98	66	29	3	2
Do homework	<11	97	80	7	10	3
	>11	94	86	6	2	6
Hang around with friends	<11	92	5	84	3	8
	>11	97	3	91	3	3
Watch videos/DVDs	<11	93	28	42	23	7
	>11	94	23	59	12	6
Go to the cinema	<11	93	3	64	26	7
	>11	95	1	85	9	5
Play team sports	<11	86	3	59	24	14
	>11	81	2	56	23	19
Read books and comics	<11	91	84	6	1	9
	>11	77	73	3	1	23
Skate/rollerblade/cycle	<11	90	23	54	13	10
	>11	78	19	52	7	22
Discos/night clubs	<11	60	2	52	6	40
	>11	72	1	64	7	28
Youth/church club	<11	52	6	33	13	48
	>11	52	3	42	7	48
Church activities	<11	55	6	27	22	45
	>11	46	3	29	14	54
Time with boy-/girlfriend	<11	33	17	14	2	67
	>11	54	29	22	3	46

Note also the activities which decreased significantly with age – reading books and comics, skate/rollerblading and church – and those which increased – discos/night clubs and boy/girl friends.

What they enjoy about such activities

Freedom to choose was the main factor, according to the Focus Group Tweenagers, followed by staving off boredom. "I'm bored" is a common cry of children, but by this age Tweenagers are beginning to know their own mind, and will choose activities they like. The nature of the activity is less important than "doing what we want", or "not being told what to do" – it is these factors which make leisure time so valuable to youngsters compared with the compulsory nature of the majority of the school day. Not surprisingly "having fun" was the other main reason. It seems that something is not worth doing unless there is the dimension of "fun" in it!

Time spent

This RAKES survey did not ask how long Tweenagers spent on their different activities, but other studies can supply that information for some of them. A third, 32%, of those aged 13 to 15 went to the cinema at least twice a month in 1999, for instance[2]; and another third, 31%, once a month; 17% went every two or three months; and 13% two or three times a year. 6% said they only went once a year, and 1% said they never went, figures broadly equating to the 6% "I don't do it" here. This works out at an average of once every three weeks.

In England in 1999 young people aged 13 to 16 watched television or video for 12.2 hours a week, did school homework for 5.7 hours, looked after younger children for 5.3 hours, played computer games for 5.1 hours, played a musical instrument for 3.9 hours, read books, magazines or comics for 3.8 hours, and did other hobbies for 7.7 hours a week[3].

Reading

There are a number of magazines aimed especially at the Tweenage market, mostly girls, including *Mizz* (for 10–13 year olds), *Mad About Boys* (for 9–13 year old girls), *Sugar* (for 11–16 year old girls and the market leader), *Elle Girl* (for 13–17 year olds) and *Cosmo Girl* (for 12–17 year olds). The majority of these magazines focus "girls' ambitions firmly on their panty line"[4]. When they graduate from these, *Live Kicks, Smash Hits, Shout, cd:uk* and *Top of the Pops* await them.

What Tweenagers read does not seem to have been greatly researched, except to note that many Tweenagers do not appear to read many books. Table 5.4 suggests that over nine-tenths do up to age 11, but after that many other activities compete, and only three-quarters, 77%, read books or comics. However, these would read half an hour a day using the above figures. "The market for teenage fiction is one of the most difficult areas of publishing to get right."[5]

There are 3 groups: those who have already become "non-readers", those who are potential readers but who are embarrassed at looking for suitable books in the children's sections of libraries or bookshops, or who would read if their confidence and learning difficulties could be overcome, and those who have well-formed reading habits who frequently read books published for the general adult market[6].

What do they read? Julie Burchill's first novel for Tweenagers, aged 12 to 16, called *Sugar Rush*. Published in February 2003, it is "a story of love between two teenage girls".[7] How typical is that type of book? Probably not typical, according to the library development agency Well Worth Reading who in partnership with the National Youth Agency is trying to encourage those aged 13 to 18 to read more books in a project called YouthBoox[8]. Another library scheme, Reading Challenge Plus, aimed at young people aged 11 to 13, is "designed to motivate them to read six books over the summer holidays"[9]. WH Smith doubled its sales of teenage titles between 2001 and 2002[10].

Tweenager fiction books advertised in the 21 September 2001 issue of *The Bookseller* included *Thursday's Child,* by Sonya Hartnett, "a slick, chilly psychological thriller"; *the mañana man,* by James Birrell, "an achingly funny novel about friendship, life, love and growing up"; *Mates, Dates and Inflatable Bras* by Cathy Hopkins, providing "interesting, zappy, funny teenage books"; *Pictures of the Night,* Adèle Geras "a loose reworking of a fairy tale"; *The Journal of Danny Chaucher (Poet)* by Roger Stevens describing "the desires and insights of a teenage boy"; and among others *Sorceress* by Celia Rees with "compelling historical episodes". If this selection is typical, these suggest a wide range but focusing on Tweenager personal issues, including sexuality, reflecting market demand. They have to be "fast-paced, very easy, fun reads" according to Emma Matthewson, editing US author Cecily von Ziegesar's *Gossip Girl* series of books for girls 14 or over[11]. Some occult books focus on this age-group, sometimes with bizarre results[12].

In 2001 children's books were dominated by the Harry Potter series, one of which was also made into a film and released in the autumn. The author, J K Rowling, made a fortune of some £25 million. Quite literally millions of her books sold, and were read by young people of all ages, equally male and female, including Tweenagers, as well as many adults also (who bought a third, 33%, of total sales!)[13]. Controversy raged in the Christian press as to whether such stories about witchcraft were wholesome or not. Good does beat evil in them. Part of this popularity was "branding", especially after the film was released, with Harry Potter being defined by his glasses! In Denmark, one 2001 survey of young people's reading habits found they had no time to read anything but textbooks – and Harry Potter[14]!

J K Rowling is not the only young people's author writing on grand themes. Philip Pullman (whose aim is "to destroy Christianity"[15]) writes equally compellingly. The first volume in his trilogy, *The Amber Spyglass,* won the Whitbread prize, and is an unstoppable read about a young girl seeking to rescue a friend kidnapped by agents of a malevolent church. In the final volume, *His Dark Materials,* he makes clear his hatred of the God of the Bible, and instead brings in angels of darkness, and more.

Likewise Cate Tiernan's *Book of Shadows,* the first of a series of seven, is about a young girl who joins a Wicca coven, learns spells and has supernatural experiences and Wicca rituals[16]. These books view "Wicca as girl power, positive, life affirming, fun, green, eco-friendly, spooky, scary/ exciting, and offer a role model of young women that many aspire to"[17].

Several publishers have launched a separate list of literary fiction for Tweenagers. Macmillan Children's Books, for example, has a separate list Young Picador[18], and another called Boxtree; HarperCollins launched CollinsFlamingo in May 2001[19]; Little, Brown have Orbit; and Time Warner began their teenage imprint, Atom, in July 2002[20]. From a Christian perspective, many suitable titles are listed in the Christian Publicity Organisation youth worker's catalogue *Sorted,* which has a wide variety of books, videos and other items[21].

Authors can start young also: Little, Brown gave a "substantial five-figure" advance to a 14 year old for two science fiction books, the first, *Mirror Dreams,* published in January 2001, the second following in 2002; their editorial staff read the script without being told the author's age[22].

Age allowed unsupervised activity

Naturally young people are allowed by their parents to do more as they get older. One study commissioned by the NSPCC sought to ascertain when unsupervised activity was first allowed[23], with the following results. The actual figures are given in Appendix 4, Table A4/8.

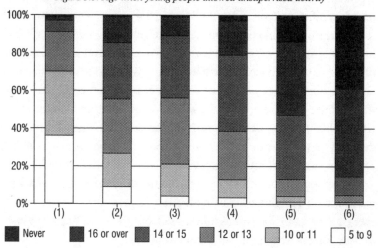

Figure 5.5: Age when young people allowed unsupervised activity

Column keys

(1) = Allowed to go to school without an adult or much older child

(2) = Allowed to go out in the evening on your own to a friend's/anywhere

(3) = Allowed to go to town centre shops without an adult or much older child

(4) = Allowed to stay at home in the evening without adult to supervise

(5) = Allowed to stay at home overnight without adult to supervise

(6) = Allowed to stay out overnight without parents knowing where you were

The average age for these activities was, respectively, 10.4, 12.8, 13.0, 13.6, 15.8 and 16.3 years, based on the proportion of the sample who gave an age in answer to the question. The survey also showed that 4% of respondents were allowed to stay out overnight without parents knowing where they were when under the age of 14[24].

Sexual activity

Britain would not have the highest rate of teenage pregnancy in Europe if much sexual activity did not take place before the age of consent of 16, although the large majority, 84% in 1999[25], of teenage pregnancies occur after that age. Since 1978 the average number of births to women under the age of 20 has been fairly static at about 30 for every 1,000 women, a rate of 3%, or 1 for every 33 young women.

The number of conceptions is larger than the number of births, however. In 1990, 45,000 women under 18 conceived a baby, a rate of 4.8%[26] or 1 for every 21 young women, of which 41% were aborted. By 2000 the number had dropped slightly to 41,000 conceptions to those under 18, a rate of 4.4%, with 43% aborted, the lowest level since 1995[27]. Many of these pregnancies are unplanned, and the decision on whether or not to have an abortion depends often on the potential support from the girl's family[28].

These abortion rates vary between the different ethnic minority groups, with Bangladeshis being highest (almost twice the national rate), followed by Pakistanis and those from the Caribbean; Indians are the lowest (less than half the national rate)[29].

The above figures include conceptions to girls under the age of 16. In 1990 there were 8,000 conceptions in this age-group, a rate of 0.95%, or 1 for every 110 girls aged 13 to 15, of which 51% were aborted. In 2000, with an increasing under-16 population in the 1990s, there were also 8,000 Tweenage conceptions, but a slightly reduced rate of 0.83%, or 1 for every 120 girls, of which 53% were aborted. This is marginally higher than the 0.82% rate in 1999.

It is important to understand what these Government figures are saying. In 1990 there were 850,000 girls aged between 13 and 15 in England, a number which had grown to 950,000 by 1999, and which is set to decline to about 870,000 by 2021. In the year 1999, 8,000 of these conceived a baby. In 2000 the number of girls aged 13 to 15 was about 950,000 and 8,000 of these will have conceived. The same will have been true in 2001. In other words, as the cohort of girls aged 13 to 15 *passed through these three years,* about 24,000 babies were conceived. While a few probably conceived more than one, in broad terms, 24,000 babies were conceived across these 950,000 girls, or 1 in every 40[30]. In a school with a Year 9 (aged 13) of say 40 girls, on average 1 will have conceived before the end of Year 11 (aged 15). This will be true for every Year 9 cohort.

Of course conception is relatively rare, even when condoms are not used (and the Government encourages their use very strongly[31]), by comparison with the number of instances of sexual intercourse. These numbers are therefore indicating only the tip of the iceberg in the amount of sexual activity at these ages.

In 1998 30% of women aged 16 to 19 indicated that they had not had a sexual partner the previous year (which is not quite the same as saying they were virgins), 37% had had one, and 33% two or more[32]. This is based on the Health Education Monitoring Survey, a Government survey undertaken by the Office for National Statistics, and therefore likely to be fairly reliable. Figures for 1999 and for girls aged 13 to 15 are not available: for those aged 16 to 19 it can be presumed the percentage not having a partner would be similar in 1999. Hopefully it would be larger for younger girls[33], say perhaps 50% or 70%. But that simply means that 50% or 30% have had a sexual partner by 15, a proportion of "almost half" which is supported by an American study[34].

The percentage rose greatly in the latter half of the 1990s: the Family Planning Association in 1994 said only 20% of under-16s had had sex,[35] but a Natsal survey in 2001 put the figure as "more than a quarter"[36]. (Perhaps up to a tenth of this is abuse within a Tweenager's home[37].) A survey in the year 2000 found that "a quarter of women and nearly a third of men have had sex under the age of 16"[38]. A 2001 survey found "26% of girls lose their virginity before the age of 16"[39]. However, an important survey by the Family Education Trust, a Christian organisation, in 2000 found a much lower percentage – 17% of under 16s had had sex[40].

This latter survey found that the percentage indicating they had had sex increased rapidly from age 13 (9%) to age 14 (18%) to age 15 (26%). When asked when they had first had sex, 1 in 7 (15%) said when 11 or younger, another 1 in 7 (16%) when 12, a third (34%) when 13, just under a third (29%) when 14 and the remaining 6% when 15[41]. Full details are given in Table A4/9. If these figures are typical, then sexual activity starts young. It is also twice as likely to happen if the Tweenager's parents are divorced, and *ten times* more likely if their friends have had sex[42].

No wonder the Government is wanting to make the morning-after pill available without prescription to women over 16, and to encourage school nurses to distribute the pill free to girls under 16 without their parents' consent! (76% of girls in one study said it would be good if this pill was easier to get hold of[43].) Hence also the Government's moves to change the age of consent. Both of these have generated much Christian opposition[44].

There is also the danger of infection: in 1998, there were 19,800 new cases of sexually transmitted diseases among women aged 16 to 19, and 1,200 of those under 16[45].

Surely, it will be said, the situation is different for Tweenagers who are Christian or who are at least part of a churchgoing family? There have been relatively few studies of sexual behaviour of church (or Christian) young people. A 1991 study of 15 to 19 year olds, many of whom were connected to a church, found that 9% of 15 year olds said they had had sexual intercourse, a percentage which rose to 43% of those aged 19[46], with an overall average of 18%. A 1997 survey which included those connected to a church aged 11 to 14 as well as those aged 15 to 19 found a lower average level, of 12%[47], but this was made up of 5% for those 15 or under and 22% for those aged 16 to 19. The older teenager percentage had thus increased from 18% to 22% in the six years 1991 to 1997. The 5% figure is smaller than the 17% figure just mentioned in the Family Education Trust study, but the first relates to 1997 and the second figure to 2000.

What this is saying is that even church-connected Tweenagers are engaging in full sexual activity, but that while the level is less than for Tweenagers generally, the amount of such activity increased, perhaps quite dramatically, over the last half of the 1990s. Dr Trevor Stammers, a GP and tutor in general practice at St George's Hospital, Tooting said that condoms are not the answer because "the pressures encouraging teenagers to have sex have probably never been greater."[48] One teenager put it, "it sometimes seems as if sex is compulsory but contraception has failed"[49].

An excellent study by The Guide Association summarised "Today's Girl" (aged 14 to 17 in this survey) as one who "feels she has greater control over her life than her mother had... *more freedom* but more responsibility."[50] A survey in a teenage magazine seemed to agree. It concluded, "While boys flounder and fret over the rules of the new sexual marketplace, girls are enjoying unprecedented *freedom* and choice in relationships."[51]

Market forces

The RAKES survey didn't ask Tweenagers if they spent any of their time shopping. Perhaps it should! As Table 5.2 indicates, 2.3% of respondents wrote in "shopping" as one of their other interests. As one national newspaper put in its headlines "Tweenagers are a cool new tribe on the streets of London. They have their own look, their own language – and plenty of their parents' money."[52]

Examples of their language were given in the same article, and are reproduced in Table 5.6, even though many of these expressions are already outmoded (!):

Table 5.6: Tweenagers talking the talk in 2000

What they say	What they mean
• He's buff	• He's cute
• You mashed your scooter? *Shame!*	• You crashed your micro-scooter? How embarrassing!
• Those CKs look like a G	• Those Calvin Klein jeans look good
• That's swanky manky	• That's disgusting (ie it hasn't got a designer label on it)
• That's well jazzy	• That's really disgusting (ie it may be second-hand)
• He dissed Destiny's Child – that's cold, man	• He criticised my favourite R&B band and I'm unimpressed

These examples indicate the importance of certain brand names. A survey of 10,000 young people aged 6 to 16 in 1997 showed that "many British teenagers consider an array of electrical goods in their bedrooms to be a necessity rather than a luxury. In his bedroom in Filton, Bristol, John Angell, 13, has a television, cassette player, personal stereo and a £150 Sony PlayStation complete with ten games costing £40 each. John takes his consumerist lifestyle for granted. 'I couldn't imagine living without my TV and PlayStation. I'm no different from other people my age – everyone's parents buy them things like this.'"[53]

A 1996 Government survey showed that on average young people aged 7 to 15 spent £8.40 a week, 38% of which went on food and drink, though this included money for school dinners. Toys, CDs and sports goods accounted for a further 19% and clothing and footwear a further 13%. The average for those aged 11 or 12 was £8.00, 13 or 14 £13.30, and 15 £16.60.[54] Five years later, in 2001, the amount spent on average had increased almost by half as much again to £12.30 a week, an increase more than three times that in the rate of inflation, with girls spending £13.20 to boys £11.20[55].

Retailers, said another report, "are fighting a losing battle to attract a fashion-conscious generation more tempted by branded sportswear."[56] Tweenagers, aged between 8 and 12, "are spending big money on the latest food, music, clothes and gadgets"[57].

Such behaviour "is surely among those absorbed at very young ages from familial examples. If parents repeatedly choose a brand, that brand appears repeatedly at home on the shelf – it is familiar – which makes it 'good'. Further, since 'father/mother knows best', brands which parents choose must be preferred over others for good reason. Advertising reinforces brand loyalty."[58]

This quotation, from a mid-1990s survey, is perhaps less true at the beginning of the 21st century, where apart from the importance of "icon" branding, the impact of new technology also makes large demands on spending by Tweenagers. In 2000, 74% of 11 to 14 year olds used the internet and 39% owned or used mobile phones.[59]

"Many teenage girls wear provocative makeup and lingerie that evoke the 'Lolita' look while others want to appear 'hip-hop' or 'glam'... Tweenage boys want to look swagger-tough while waiting for their voices to change. Tweenagers are experiencing too much 'superficial sophistication' because the freedom they are given to make choices and have their opinions heard gives them a false sense of power that will not translate to the real world. Consequently, these young adult wannabes, spoiled and self-centred, may never really learn to grow up."[60]

"Hip-hop is not just about a type of music. It's about lifestyle. It had its origins among urban youth and addresses their fashions, language, art and attitudes... In many ways it represents reality for urban youth, or at least their perceived reality. The lyrics of many hip-hop artists glorify sex, violence and misogyny. Rape, murder and gang life are common themes. Sadly, many kids – even in the church – are in love with hip-hop."[61]

It is clear that market forces affect Tweenagers strongly, and Christian Tweenagers also. One of the top trends of the new millennium was stated as "marketers are aggressively seeking out teenagers in a pre-emptive strike to capture their hearts, minds – and wallets."[62] Gary Ruskin in an article went further – "if you own this child at an early age, you can own this child for years to come"[63]. However, "most teenagers know when they're being exploited, and it's more likely that soliciting input from young people will create a population of savvier consumers. That can't be all bad."[64] While these comments come from America, they are undoubtedly true of British teenagers too.

Youth Clubs

A further question on the RAKES form asked respondents if they attended any of a range of activities in a church hall during the week. A third, 34%, said NO, but the other two-thirds, 66%, did, ranged as follows:

- 20% Sunday School/Junior Church
- 19% Youth Club
- 19% Youth group/fellowship
- 14% Out-of-school clubs
- 13% Scouts/Guides
- 12% Drama/music groups
- 9% Holiday clubs
- 6% Campaigners/Crusaders/Pathfinders
- 5% Boys/Girls' Brigade, and
- 4% Rock Solid Clubs.

In addition, 4% went to other activities not listed. On average, if a Tweenager attended at least one of these, they attended two of them. Attendance did relate, however, to whether or not a Tweenager had ever gone to church or Sunday School (Figure 5.7) and by their age (Figures 5.8 and 5.9) as the following diagrams show. Numerical details for Figures 5.7, 5.8 and 5.9 are given in Appendix 4, Tables A4/10 and 11.

Figure 5.7: Attendance at weekly church activities by church attendance

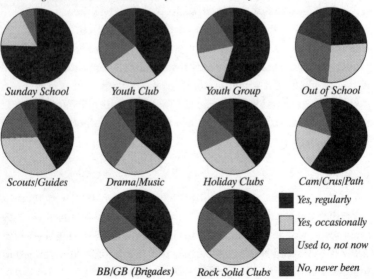

| Sunday School | Youth Club | Youth Group | Out of School |

| Scouts/Guides | Drama/Music | Holiday Clubs | Cam/Crus/Path |

| BB/GB (Brigades) | Rock Solid Clubs |

■ *Yes, regularly*
▢ *Yes, occasionally*
▨ *Used to, not now*
■ *No, never been*

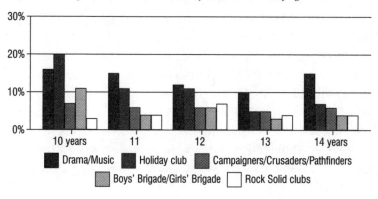

Figure 5.8: Attendance at weekly church activities by age

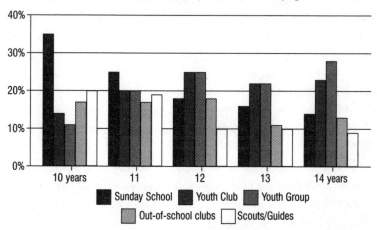

Figure 5.9: Attendance at weekly church activities by age

These diagrams show that some activities appeal more to those who regularly or occasionally attend church – Sunday School as would otherwise be expected, but Holiday Clubs and Campaigners/ Crusaders/Pathfinders also. Other activities appeal to those who go to church, especially when they run as church activities, but also to those who have stopped going or who have never been to church. Boys' and Girls' Brigades and Rock Solid Clubs are examples of these.

Likewise some activities appeal more to younger Tweenagers than older. Sunday School is one of these, and so are Holiday Clubs, the Boys' and Girls' Brigades[65] and Scouts and Guides. Others seems to attract young people at all ages – Campaigners, Crusaders and Pathfinders do this. Others attract those more in specific years – the Rock Solid Clubs do this for young people in Year 8, their second year in secondary school when they are about the age of 12. Some are more attractive to older youngsters, like Youth Groups.

Only one of these activities were more likely to be attended by girls rather than boys – drama and music groups, at which girls outnumbered boys by 2:1.

Those who attend some of these activities regularly have stronger beliefs than those who do not. Details are in Table A4/12, and show that those attending Sunday School, Youth Groups (but not youth clubs), Campaigners/Crusaders/Pathfinders and drama and music groups have a significantly higher likelihood of believing in God, Heaven or Jesus. Youth clubs do not appear to help with belief in God, Holiday Clubs with belief in Jesus or Boys'/Girls' Brigades with belief in Heaven!

What are these activities like? A third, 33%, described them as "excellent", almost half, 48%, as "good", a seventh, 14%, as "average" and 5% as "poor".

It would seem that those attending Sunday School and Holiday Clubs regularly were marginally more likely to get mostly A grades at school (46% and 45% respectively) than those who did not attend (32% and 34% respectively).

Some attended other activities – air or army cadets, basketball, choir (0.5%), Christian Union, coffee mornings, ballet/dancing (1%), debating club, football club (1%), martial arts/karate, netball, sports clubs (0.5%), St John's ambulance, table tennis, tennis, youth Alpha, etc.

So what does all this mean?

This chapter has shown:
- Some activities are so universal among Tweenagers that they can be considered as virtually mandatory for this age-group – watching television, listening to music, doing homework, hanging around with friends, watching videos/DVDs, going to the cinema and playing home computer/electronic games.
- While some of these activities, like homework, are mostly solitary occupations, Tweenagers much prefer activities which they can do with others. This may reflect in part their normal development over these years.
- While still at junior school, children frequently undertake activities with parents and other relatives, but after a year or so in secondary school, their friends play a major and increasingly important part in their lives. Could this be true not just of the things they do together, but their beliefs and moral values also?
- Tweenagers are an extremely creative and curious group, undertaking activities of all kinds, both outdoors and indoors.
- Sport and dancing activities are very popular – both are non-solo and high energy. Do church activities need to be similar to attract them?
- The most popular male activities are playing electronic games, watching videos, going to the cinema and hanging around with friends. The most popular female activities are hanging around with friends, going to the cinema and watching videos (both lists in order).
- Three activities increased with age – homework, discos/night clubs and spending time with a boy/girl friend. Those which decreased with age were reading books and comics, skate/rollerblading and going to church.
- Although not all Tweenagers read, for those that do there is an increasingly competitive market place of fiction books published just for them.

- Those aged 14 or over are increasingly allowed to stay at home alone in the evening, stay at home overnight without an adult to supervise or to stay out overnight without parents knowing where they are, though one-third, 36%, of parents forbade the last at any age.

- There is a vast amount of sexual activity among Tweenagers, a small proportion of which leads to a baby being conceived, half of which are aborted. It would seem that this activity increases from low levels at 12 years of age to much higher levels over the next three years, so that by the age of 16 only 30% at most still have their virginity. It would also appear that these levels of intercourse accelerated in the last five years of the 20th century.

- Tweenagers form a niche market which many commercial organisations target. To have, hold or wear the right "icon" is desirable for many Tweenagers.

- Two-thirds of Tweenagers go to midweek "club" activity usually in a church hall. Some of these activities are explicitly Christian, and some are better at reaching non-church Tweenagers than others. Sunday school is mostly attended by churchgoers, but Rock Solid Clubs which are being delivered jointly by Youth for Christ and Crusaders, for example, attract a relatively high proportion of non-churchgoers. The attractiveness of these activities varies with age, generally becoming less desirable the older a Tweenager.

NOTES

[1] *Reaching and Keeping Teenagers,* Peter Brierley, Monarch Publications, Crowborough, 1992, Page 123.

[2] Cinema attendance by age, 1999, Table 5.8, *Social Focus on Young People,* National Statistics, the Stationery Office, 2000.

[3] Ibid., Figure 5.1.

[4] Article "Sex, boys and make-up: is this what tweenie girls want?" by Sandra Barwick in the *Daily Telegraph,* 8 February 2001, Page 22.

[5] Article "A teen dream" by Joanne Owen in *The Bookseller,* 21 September 2001, Page 38.

[6] Ibid.

[7] Macmillan Children's Books, as noted in *The Bookseller,* 23 November 2001, Page 31.

[8] Article "Switch on to reading" by Miranda McKearney in *record,* The Library Association, September 2001, Volume 103, Number 9, Page 551.

[9] Article "Libraries challenge teens" in *The Bookseller,* 10 August 2001, Page 32.

[10] Article "Teenage market in turmoil" by Caroline Horn in *The Bookseller,* 17 May 2002, Page 14.

[11] Article "Protests at sex and drugs in teen publishing sensation" by James Morrison, in the *Independent* on Sunday, 25 August 2002.

[12] See, for example, *What on earth are we doing to our children?,* an appeal to the nation's conscience by the Maranatha Community, March 1995, Page 37.

[13] Short article in *The Bookseller,* 11 May 2001, Page 7.

[14] Short article by Michael de Laine in *The Bookseller,* 15 June 2001, Page 9.

[15] Article "Poisoned pen?", Mark Greene, *Christianity+Renewal,* London, April 2002, Page 70.

[16] Editorial by John Buckeridge, *Christianity+Renewal,* London, April 2002, Page 11. Cate Tiernan's series was published by Puffin, London, February – September, 2002, one a month.

[17] Personal correspondence with John Buckeridge, 4 April 2002.

[18] News item in *The Bookseller,* 13 April 2001, Page 31.

[19] News item in *The Bookseller,* 9 February 2001, Page 39.

[20] News item in *The Bookseller,* 17 May 2002, Page 36.

[21] Available from sorted@cpo.org.uk or from SORTED@CPO, Garcia Estate, Canterbury Road, Worthing, West Sussex BN13 1BW.

[22] Article "Just to cheer her on" in *The Bookseller,* 9 February 2001, Page 36.

[23] Article "The prevalence of child abuse and neglect: a survey of young people" by Sue Brooker, Pat Cawson, Graham Kelly and Corinne Wattam, winner of the Application of Research Award, *International Journal of Market Research,* Volume 43, Quarter 3, 2001, Page 249.

[24] Ibid., Page 271.

[25] Report in *Population Trends,* National Statistics, The Stationery Office, Norwich, Number 106, Winter 2001, Page 72.

[26] Based on the number of women aged 15 to 17.

[27] Article "Schoolgirl pregnancies raise safe sex fears" in the *Daily Telegraph,* 1 March 2002, Page 13.

[28] Report "What influences teenagers' decisions about unplanned pregnancy?" in *Findings,* Joseph Rowntree Foundation, November 2000, www.jrf.org.uk

[29] Article "Teenage births to ethnic minority women" by Richard Berthoud in *Population Trends,* Office for National Statistics, Number 104, Summer 2001, Page 12.

[30] When the calculations are done more exactly to one decimal place, this figure is unchanged. It is actually 39.9.

[31] Some argue that this just makes things worse. See, for example, Tom Utley's article "Handing out condoms will encourage teenage sex" in the *Daily Telegraph,* 29 June 2002, Page 22.

[32] *Social Focus on Young People,* Office for National Statistics, The Stationery Office, Norwich, 2000, Table 2.26. For young men aged 16 to 19, the percentages were 48% none, 24% one, and 28% two or more.

[33] Few figures are available. An article in the *Daily Mail* on 6 January 2001, put the figure in 1990 as "just over three-quarters", but virginity has rapidly decreased in the 1990s and this figure is not an accurate guide for the end-1990s.

[34] Article in *Psychology Today,* Nov/Dec 2000, Page 10, via www.navpress.com, June 2001. There was an additional comment: "Of those [having sex], slightly more than half of the boys regret that decision as do almost three out of four girls."

[35] Article "Teenage Sexuality" by Steve Chalke in *Renewal,* December 1994, Page 38.

[36] Article "A taste of the hard-core curriculum" by Cassandra Jardine in the *Daily Telegraph,* 2nd January, 2002, Page 15.

[37] Op. cit., (Footnote 23), Table 7. Of the under 16s, 2% had had full sexual intercourse always or sometimes against their wishes (1% male, 3% female), and 4% with someone five or more years older (2% male, 6% female) in a presumed home context.

[38] *Sex at the Millennium,* part of a "National Strategy for Sexual Health and HIV" by Professors Anne Johnson and Michael Adler, University College London, and described in *UCL People,* Spring 2002, Page 43.

[39] *National Survey of Sexual Attitudes and Lifestyles 1999–2001,* reported in *Sociology Update* 2002, Professor Martyn Denscombe, Page 35. He also reported that the same survey found that "four out of five girls who first had sex at 13 or 14 regretted it".

[40] *Sex under Sixteen?,* Rev Dr Clifford Hill, Family Education Trust, London, 2000, Page 48. The 17% would rise to 18% if those who answered "don't know" were distributed in the same proportions as those who did.

[41] Ibid., taking figures from Page 18, and Figures 25 and 26.

[42] Ibid., Figure 25.

[43] *Today's Girl, Tomorrow's Woman,* A special report, The Guide Association, London, 2000, Page 13. Details from www.guides.org.uk

[44] See, for example, *The morning after pill, Promoting Promiscuity,* and *Age of consent: the case against change,* both by The Christian Institute, Newcastle upon Tyne, January 2001, and March 1999 respectively, and accompanying Press Releases.

[45] Op. cit., (Footnote 32), Table 2.17. For men the figures are 6,400 for those aged 16 to 19, and 200 for those under 16.

[46] *Reaching and Keeping Teenagers,* Peter Brierley, Monarch Publications, 1993, Table 13, Page 76.

[47] Survey for Agapé, as published in *Quadrant,* Christian Research, Autumn 1997, Page 3.

[48] Article "Parenting Today", *Baptist Times,* 28 October 1999, Page 7.

[49] Article "Britain second worst country for schoolgirl pregnancies" by Sarah Womack, *Daily Telegraph,* 30 May 2002, Page 8.

[50] Op. cit., (Footnote 43), Page 4 [my italics].

[51] Article in *The Face,* No 66, July 2002, Page 69 [my italics].

[52] Features in the *Evening Standard,* 29 August 2000, Page 23.

[53] Article "Materialism rules for Britain's teens" by Nicholas Hellen and Andrew Alderson, *The Sunday Times,* 8 March 1998, Page 4.

[54] *Children's Spending,* 1995–96, Office for National Statistics, London, 22 July 1997.

[55] The Office of National Statistics study, from a report in the *Daily Telegraph* 1 August, 2002.

[56] Article "Sporty children fill wardrobe with Nike, not Next" by Clifford German, *The Independent,* 7 April 1997, Page 6.

[57] Article "Glitter Babes, Geri and WWF. Welcome to the teenage world" by David Lister in *The Independent,* 29 May 2001.

[58] Article "Reliance on brand by young children" by Cynthia and Robert Hite, *Journal of the Market Research Society,* Volume 37, Number 2, April 1995, Page 187.

[59] Article "Selling more, selling better" by Caroline Horn in *The Bookseller,* 13 April 2001, Page 32.

[60] Article "The truth about tweens" by Barbara Kantrowitz and Pat Wingert in *Newsweek,* 18 October 1999, Volume 134, Number 16, Page 62.

[61] Article "Hip-hop kingdom come" by William Brown and Benson Fraser, *Christianity Today,* 8 January 2001, Volume 45, Number 1, Page 48.

[62] Top Trends of the New Millennium, by the editors of *The Trend Letter,* Briefings Publishing Group, Alexandria, Virginia, United States, 2001, Page 5.

[63] Article "Why they whine: How Corporations prey on children" by Gary Ruskin in *Mothering* magazine, November/December 1999, Page 42, and quoted in *Living on Purpose,* Tom and Christine Sine, Monarch Books, London, 2002, Page 29.

[64] Ibid., Page 8.

[65] The actual membership of Girls' Brigades peaks at 8 years of age. See the graph of Figure 5.8.2 in *Religious Trends* No 3, 2002/2003, edited Peter Brierley, Christian Research, 2001.

The experience of church

The Strathspey Railway is a small privately owned steam line which runs from Aviemore to Broomhill in Scotland, on which I travelled in August 2002 while on holiday. It was nostalgic to be back in the days when steam trains ran.

Talking afterwards to one of the volunteer workers who helped to make the line function I realised that this was a venture under severe threat. The youngest people who can remember steam engines from personal travel experience are now in their early 40s. Membership of the various steam train societies dotted around the UK are almost entirely made up from those in their 40s, 50s and especially in their 60s. They find recruiting younger people extremely difficult, as they simply haven't had such travel experience.

Why should younger people join? A few might join out of curiosity, but their interest is often fleeting, and they leave after a year or so. It is simply an outmoded method of transport.

The same can so easily become true of the church. Unless our young people experience worship, they can easily grow up never having been inside a church apart from perhaps for a wedding or a funeral. Could the church become as irrelevant as the steam train? Important for an older age, nice to experience occasionally, but not relevant to the 21st century?

Tweenagers and their experience of church

Almost a quarter of the questions on the form concerned Tweenagers' experiences of and attitudes towards church. The survey showed that 36% of this sample said they went to church regularly (although regularity was not defined), 18% said they went occasionally, 22% said they used to attend but didn't now (lapsed), and 24% said they had never gone. Questions were asked to explore relevant issues for each of these groups as well as additional general issues.

Tweenagers' experience of church varied by the grades they mostly received for their school work, and by gender, as Table 6.1 shows. This Table gives an overview of the four levels at which churchgoing was measured which are then considered in more detail:

Table 6.1: Experience of church by school grade

Usual Grade	Regular %	Occasional %	Lapsed %	Never %	Base
Mostly As	46	18	19	17	626
Mostly Bs	28	19	25	28	942
Mostly Cs	24	17	25	34	235
Mostly Ds–Fs	20	28	26	26	35
Overall	36	18	22	24	2,019
Male	32	20	19	29	935
Female	40	17	24	19	1,084

This Table shows that those going to church regularly are likely to achieve higher grades at school, whereas those going occasionally or not at all achieve lower grades[1]. Girls were more likely to be at church regularly or no longer, boys occasionally or never.

Main reasons why Tweenagers don't go to church

"Many young people your age do not go to church, and others have stopped going. Why do you think that is?" No fewer than 22 reasons were suggested, with an open box as well. On average each respondent ticked nine boxes. Six reasons were ticked by a majority of respondents.

- 87% They think it is boring   [89%]
- 73% They think going to church isn't cool   [60%]
- 67% They can't be bothered   [—]
- 64% They don't believe in God   [57%]
- 63% They've got other things to do on a Sunday   [48%]
- 61% None of their friends go   [58%]

This list is almost identical to the results of asking teenagers aged 11 to 18 in 1992, and the figures in square brackets at the end of each line give the percentage response in that study for those aged 11 to 14.[2] "They can't be bothered" wasn't an option in that study.

This is an interesting list. Only one of these, the first, relates to church as such at all. Tweenagers perceive church as a boring experience, something not on their wavelength. This is partly because "young people are looking for a place where they are listened to, where they are treated as a human being and where they have room to make their own space"[3], and as church usually does not provide this, they have to fit into the existing patterns, which they find "boring" because they are outside their experience.

Four of these reasons are to do with themselves or their friends: it isn't cool (as judged by their friends' reactions), their friends don't go, they can't be bothered (or perhaps don't see the necessity) or don't have time (clash of priorities). As if to justify these personal reasons they say they don't believe in God, assuming that belief in God equates with church attendance.

The largest differences between 1992 and 2001 is in Tweenagers having other things to do, followed by it not being cool. In the nine years separating these two studies, the nature of Sunday has changed considerably, with much more Sunday sport and the introduction of Sunday shopping. It would seem that peer pressure is also greater than it was for this age-group. The overall figure of 63% is a little lower than a survey in 2000 by Youth for Christ of over 50 youth leaders, who said that over three-quarters of young people were "simply too busy to go to church on Sundays"[4].

Some of these answers varied by the age or school year of a

Tweenager. Not believing in God did not vary by school year (as if once having made up their mind, the issue was fixed), but the other reasons did, as shown in Table 6.2.

Table 6.2: Reasons for non-attendance at church by age

Reason	10 yrs %	11 yrs %	12 yrs %	13 yrs %	14 yrs %	Overall %
They think it is boring	74	88	89	89	92	87
It isn't cool	60	74	79	76	75	73
They can't be bothered	54	71	72	67	72	67
Other things to do	54	61	64	68	69	63
None of their friends go	48	60	63	65	66	61
Average of the above	58	71	73	73	75	70
Base	365	423	480	461	337	2,066

Table 6.2 shows that most of the reasons are cited more often the older a Tweenager becomes. Only its not "being cool" drops off slightly. There is, however, a remarkable uniformity of answers for those 11 to 14, and the average difference between those 10 and those 11, 13%, is much greater than between any subsequent years. In other words, these reasons are less often given for those who are 10 years old, but once they become 11 (usually their year of entering secondary school) the numbers giving these reasons all increase and vary little after that. In this transition, this "growing up", church becomes less important and relevant and going less desirable.

Those thinking that going to church wasn't cool (alone of the six reasons given) also varied by their usual school grades. For those who mostly got grade A it wasn't cool for 79%, for grade B 74%, for grade C 64%, and for grades below C 56%. So it was felt not to be cool the higher the normal grade achieved.

This factor alone also varied by gender: 69% of boys said that going to church wasn't cool, but 77% of girls.

Other reasons why Tweenagers don't go to church

The six main reasons given for not going to church were followed by seven which were important to between a third and a half of respondents, and if these were asked in 1992 those percentages are given:

- 49% They don't get up early enough on Sundays   [—]
- 48% Their parents don't encourage them to go   [52%]
- 43% They have never thought about it   [—]
- 41% They don't know anyone at church   [15%]
- 39% They think it is irrelevant   [22%]
- 34% They don't know what happens at church   [25%]
- 33% They feel out of place   [21%]

The largest percentage jump here by far is in the fourth line "they don't know anyone at church". This would be overcome if Tweenagers came to church as a "gang": they like acting as a crowd and doing things together today. Church is increasingly seen as irrelevant, they are ignorant of what happens, and consequently would feel totally out of place. They need friends to go with, a reason for going, and a knowledge of what it's like. It is also clear that their image of church is not positive: it isn't cool, it's boring and irrelevant, and they don't know what goes on there.

Four of these reasons also varied significantly by age, as given in Table 6.3:

Table 6.3: Secondary reasons for non-attendance at church by age

Reason	10 yrs %	11 yrs %	12 yrs %	13 yrs %	14 yrs %	Overall %
Don't get up early enough	37	46	55	51	55	49
No parental encouragement	40	48	48	50	53	48
It is irrelevant	24	36	40	45	48	39
They feel out of place	19	26	37	37	46	33
Average of the above	30	39	45	46	51	42

While these four reasons generally became more important as Tweenagers got older (there is a small blip for the first at age 13), the break point of 11 years of age was less pronounced, although still the largest jump in the average figures. These reasons became more important as Tweenagers got older, and not just through the change from being 10 to being 11.

Parents not encouraging Tweenagers to go to church also varied by the grades mostly achieved. For those who usually got grade A it was 53%, grade B 48%, grade C 38% and grades below C 34%, showing that parental support was more important for those likely to get higher grades.

Getting up early enough (or perhaps not early enough!) varied by gender: it was ticked by 43% of boys but by 54% of girls.

Finally there were nine reasons which were indicated by less than a quarter of respondents, only two of which (moral teaching, and parents not liking the minister) increased with age:

- 23% They don't like the people who do go   [9%]
- 23% They go to see the parent they don't live with   [—]
- 22% They don't like the moral teaching   [14%]
- 18% They go out with their parents   [—]
- 17% They don't feel welcome   [10%]
- 16% Their families have moved away   [—]
- 15% Their parents might not like the minister/vicar   [—]
- 14% They don't like the minister/vicar   [3%]
- 11% They go out with their grandparents   [—]

Where questions were repeated across the two surveys, the latest percentages show an increasing hostility towards the church. These may be the lower percentages but the increase is quite large across nine years, and suggests it may continue to grow.

These percentages did not vary by grades normally achieved or gender. However, the first, "They don't like the people who do go", had one very different answer for those who are no longer Christian, 45% of whom ticked this box. In other words, one reason why some young people no longer go to church is because they didn't like the people who went already. This reflects the finding in a Church of Scotland survey where youth workers gave the attitude of other churchgoers as the main reason why this age group leave church[5].

A small number, 6%, gave other reasons for not going to church. These centred around their parents not being very keen, their friends ridiculing them, wanting to play football/watch video etc., thinking religion is silly or old-fashioned, or just being too lazy.

It should be possible to overcome some of the ignorance shown in these answers with appropriate teaching, given a suitable opportunity. They show the value of the church reaching out to Tweenagers, welcoming every opportunity to meet them, generally sharing their faith. So ministers and youth workers leading helpful school assemblies, for instance, could form one way of the church moving out into the world.

However, note also the percentage who go out on a Sunday, with parents or grandparents, or who go to see the parent they don't live with. This suggests the value of having midweek meetings for young people if Sunday is so busy for Tweenagers.

Focus Group responses

The churchgoing Focus Group were asked why they thought their school friends did not attend. Their answers mostly reflected those already considered in this chapter such as, "They think it's boring", or "It's not cool". They all agreed with one of the group who said, "If you haven't been you don't know what it's like". However, they gave two other responses: a fairly flippant one, "It's too cold in the winter", and a more thoughtful one, "They haven't been brought up to it and if your parents don't think it's worth going, why should you."

Most of them had told their friends that they went to church. What their friends thought about it did not seem to matter much: "Some think it's good, others think it's bad". As church is something Tweenagers do in their leisure time it was seen as a personal choice which was irrelevant at school.

All the non-churchgoing Group had been to church for a wedding, a christening, Guides/Brownies or Scout/Cubs parade, school Harvest Festival, or at Christmas. They were therefore asked what they thought of the building, the people and what happened there.

- The *building* was "old, very echoey and had lots of nice stuff inside it", it was "sort of quiet in a funny kind of way", "very grand and highly decorated".
- The *people* were "dressed up weird – why do they have to wear that stuff to sing?".
- The *event* was "well-organised", but "everyone's very serious", "no one laughs". They "use lots of funny words which they don't explain – I don't get it".

It was clear that the churches they had been to felt like another world which had not been explained to them. When asked whether they would go again, they could not see why they should get up early on a Sunday morning to go to something they did not understand.

No longer going to church

Just over a fifth of respondents, 478, indicated that they used to go to church but no longer attended. Of these, 91% gave the age at which they stopped, which is graphed in Figure 6.4:

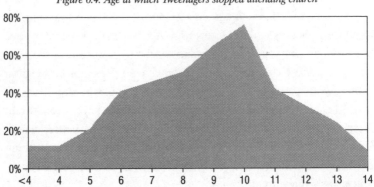

Figure 6.4: Age at which Tweenagers stopped attending church

Figure 6.4 is very clear "the majority of young people who used to go to church but no longer do so stopped between their 10th and 11th birthday "the year when the majority move to secondary school[6]. While the peak in the diagram is clear, it should be noted that 20% stop before their 7th birthday, 22% before their 9th birthday, and 15% before their 10th birthday. So nearly three-fifths, 57%, have left church before they leave junior school. One-sixth, 18%, leave before their 11th birthday, 17% before their 13th birthday, and 8% after their 13th birthday. **The key years are between the ages of 7 and 10** when young people will decide whether or not church is for them.

For how long did those who had left come? Details are given in Table A4/13 in Appendix 4, but the average was five years. This varied greatly, however, by the age at which a respondent started coming to church as Figure 6.5 shows, with a big blip for children joining when 5 or 6 and leaving when they reached secondary age.

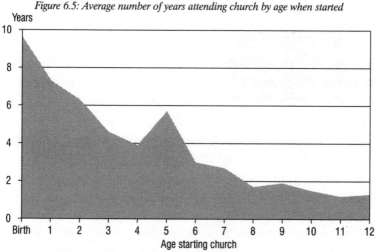

Figure 6.5: Average number of years attending church by age when started

The graph shows that those starting church between 7 and 10 are likely to only stay one or two years if they don't become committed churchgoers. The graph also shows the relatively large number of children who join "crèche" at 3 or under, many of whom will continue to stay in church for Sunday School. It is therefore especially worrying that 41% of English churches had no children of creche age in 1998[7].

On average children began attending church when about 4 years old. Young people most likely to get the highest grades at school were likely to start earlier, about 3 years of age, implying that they come with their family. Those getting Grades C to F start later, at about 5 years of age, or when they start school, which makes one wonder what brings them then.

Why did Tweenagers stop going to church? Respondents gave three reasons on average. The top five answers were straightforward:

- Virtually half, 46%, said they did not enjoy it,
- Almost as many, 44%, said they grew out of it,
- Three-eighths, 37%, said the worship service was boring,
- A quarter, 23%, said the services were old-fashioned, and
- Another quarter, 23%, said there were few other people there of their age.

The first four of these might perhaps be collectively summarised as "Church was not relevant or interesting", and was the reason cited by the one Tweenager in the non-churchgoing Focus Group who had attended church for a while. The fifth relates to the importance of having other young people around. These reasons emphasise, however, the critical importance of the way Sunday School and other activities like All Age Services are held and taught for those aged 7 to 10 years[8]. Their reactions to Sunday School at that age form the basis of their subsequent involvement or non-involvement with church (and perhaps Christianity?).

Part of the success or otherwise of such Sunday School will be the relationship between the child and the teacher. Rota teaching, exacerbated by parents attending church less frequently than weekly (with consequential irregular attendance by children), mean that that relationship is much harder to form and develop. The emphasis of Bill Wilson's Metro Church Sunday School[9] on personal visitation of every child every week helps to overcome this.

There were a number of minor reasons for stopping:

- 18% There were no activities for young people
- 17% Church services started too early
- 12% Had serious doubts about the Christian religion
- 12% Did not understand the lessons
- 11% Moved out of the area
- 10% Friends stopped going
- 9% Did not get on with other young people/children
- 8% The congregation was not welcoming
- 7% Family pressure
- 7% Did not get on with the leaders
- 7% Didn't like the way I was treated
- 4% Started going to see the parent I don't live with
- 4% Was always late
- 3% The services were too lively.

The percentage who left because they moved out of the area, 11%, is only a fifth of the adults who leave because they move[10], suggesting that parents with younger children move less frequently than those without them. This is as might be expected, but gives churches a longer opportunity for influencing them.

There were also a number giving other reasons. One in six of these was because they started playing rugby or football or other sport. Nine said, "My parents stopped going", and six said, "I only went with Gran". Nine said they only went because of Brownies, etc. and stopped when they left. Five stopped because they started secondary school with lots of homework. Six repeated the statement that it was boring. Five left because the church was too far away and they couldn't afford the transport. There were a few who gave personal reasons:

- After Dad's funeral I couldn't go into another church
- I became involved with the occult
- My sister stopped going
- I had to leave because I was too old(!)
- We started up a small group at home.

The importance of determining these reasons has been emphasised by others. "I want Christians to understand the severity of the
crisis," said Dr Roger Dudley, director of the Institute of Church
Ministry at Andrews University, in Michigan, United States, after a
studying a group of Seventh-Day Adventist youth over a 10 year
period[11].

The churchgoing Focus Group was asked why they did go to
church and these were their responses, compared with those from
the Scottish Tweenagers:

	English	Scottish
I want to learn about the Christian faith	10	1
I like being part of the group	8	7
I like the activities	9	6
My parents bring me	7	2
I have always gone	7	3
I like the leader	6	1
I want to be with friends	3	9

The English group wanted to add another factor, "I would have
a guilty conscience if I didn't go" and five of them agreed with that.

They were then asked if they had ever thought of stopping
going to church. Surprisingly two of them had already stopped and
come back again! One Tweenager's family had moved house and she
didn't like the new church they chose because she was "not involved
in anything". However, after a while she had decided to go with
them. One of the boys had stopped because of football on a Sunday
morning.

They were also asked if they thought they would still be going
to church by the time they left school. Several boys thought they
were likely to stop going to church in order to play football on
Sunday. It wasn't that they wanted to stop going to church, it was
that football was more important to them; they didn't want to give
up their faith, but it didn't fit in with their lifestyle.

One response showed the importance of the example set by the family: "My Dad doesn't go and my brother has stopped, so I expect I'll stop going too". Two considered it likely that when they were old enough to have a part-time job at the weekend they would either be working on a Sunday or doing homework having worked on Saturday. Two more raised the factor of choice: one said she was likely "to choose not to go", another said she would attend when she felt like it.

Staying in bed on a Sunday morning was something all of them agreed with, even those who intended to still attend. Most of these responses are not to do with church itself but with the time when it takes place, underlining the need to consider providing something at church for these youngsters at other times of the week.

Occasional churchgoers

One sixth, 18%, of these Tweenage respondents said they went to church occasionally. What kinds of services did they attend? Seven answers were ticked between every two respondents on average. Five in every eight, 62%, had attended for weddings or funerals, and almost half, 49%, for christenings, baptisms or dedications. But although many Tweenagers had experienced these types of services, the actual number they attended in a year was relatively small. So, the Occasional Offices, as Anglicans title these services, were the reason for just a third of these occasional visits.

The remainder attended for special types of worship services:
- 38% Christmas day/midnight mass
- 34% Carol service
- 34% Easter Day
- 24% Harvest Festival
- 23% Mothering Sunday
- 20% Youth Service
- 18% Confirmation
- 17% Church parade
- 24% Other services

The major Christian festivals drew many occasional Tweenagers to church. How may these services be used to encourage them to come on other Sundays? Were they especially attracted by the music, the festivity, the joy, the fact that larger numbers would be present? Or is it a family tradition to go to such events?

The major reasons why some Tweenagers occasionally went to church are summarised in Figure 6.6, which shows they are virtually equally spread between Occasional Offices, the major Festivals, and other services (the last 3 in the above list).

Figure 6.6: Types of services attended by those going to church occasionally

Occasional offices 32%   Festival services 38%   Other services 30%

The "other services" included normal Sunday services (26%), school chapel (22%), festivals (10%), when singing in the choir (8%), parade or family services (7%), when with grandparents (7%), other special services, like Remembrance Day, saints days, Father's Day, Sunday School Anniversary (7%), when going with a friend or relative (5%), on their birthday (3%), or if there was no football on (3%). Sadly, 2% said "I am forced to go."

Going to church

Over a third of respondents, 36%, went to church regularly, although the actual frequency was not requested. Why had they started going? Two-thirds, 65%, gave a ready answer: "My parents took me to church as a baby because they go there". Parental example was far and away the main reason why Tweenagers who went to church regularly began the habit.

Other reasons were therefore minor: 5% went because their friends went and asked them to go with them, 5% went to church because of a church activity, 4% because their parents took them to Sunday School even though they didn't go to church themselves, 3% went initially with their grandparents, and 3% went because they were curious about what went on at church. Those giving other reasons, 6%, mostly replicated answers already given with respect to parental or foster-parental influence (which didn't always start when the child was a baby), or to particular activities (choir, youth club, or Brownies, for example), or simply to "learn about religion". Some 8% didn't know why they had started going to church.

It is interesting that the influence of grandparents creeps in here also. Grandparents provide an important value system to many young people, who recognise their influence in small but steady numbers. How can the church best encourage grandparents to keep on keeping on in this way?

Why did Tweenagers go to church themselves, or think others went? They could tick as many answers as they wished, and on average the majority chose five reasons:

- 72% They have always gone
- 67% To learn about God and Jesus
- 64% They enjoy it
- 60% Their parents/family go
- 56% Their parents send them

and there were five minority reasons:

- 43% Because they think they should
- 40% To meet their friends
- 26% To sing hymns
- 24% To get points for their church youth activity
- 17% It's near home.

A few gave other reasons. Positive ones included "because it's fun", "they believe in God", "to worship God", "it comforts them" or "because they like the vicar". Negative ones included "churchgoers are insane", "they're forced to go" or because of "the food and drink".

Those who thought that young people went to church because they had always gone varied by the school grades they usually obtained. Three-quarters, 77%, of those getting grade A said they had always gone, compared with 71% getting grade B, 66% getting grade C, and 59% of those getting lower grades.

Some of these reasons also varied with age. Details are given in Table A4/15. They show that the older they are the more young people think some have gone to church because they've always gone or because their parents send them, while the older they are the less they think Tweenagers enjoy it or go to sing hymns.

The above percentages also varied according to whether the responding Tweenager was or was not a Christian. The top three reasons for going to church as given above were agreed by those who were sure they were Christians and also by those who weren't sure. But those who were no longer Christian had this order:

- 64% They've always gone
- 60% Their parents/family go
- 56% Their parents send them
- 50% To learn about God and Jesus
- 42% They enjoy it.

The enjoyment factor is much lower, and parental influence much higher. These findings are similar to a 1992 study of teenagers[12]. It was also the same in this RAKES study for those who were not Christian, including the non-churchgoers in the Focus Group. When asked why they thought some young people of their age went to church they said they "come from Christian families so their parents take them and they don't think about it".

The one who had attended for a while disagreed, saying that the friend who had taken her to church did believe it and went because she wanted to, showing the different attitude of a young person who knows a churchgoer well. Interestingly one Tweenager said a friend of hers goes because her grandfather takes her – a factor which occurs in several places in the questionnaire responses. They were curiously indifferent when asked what they would think if one of their friends started going to church, saying that if the friend wanted to go that was OK, it was her/his decision.

In other words those who had left the church or have never been connected to it do not see how churchgoing can be enjoyed and assume that young people must go because their parents make them. The reality is that churchgoers do enjoy it and, more importantly, they go because they want to learn about God and Jesus. It is the privilege (and pressure) of a divine relationship that those outside the church miss. Those who attend church regularly go for all the main reasons given above and to meet their friends (57%); human and divine relationships go together.

Denominational differences

What was the denomination of the church Tweenagers in the survey attended?
- 48% were Church of England
- 10% Baptist
- 9% Methodist
- 6% Roman Catholic
- 2% Pentecostal
- 2% House/New Church
- 2% Independent
- 8% Other denominations, and
- 13% Didn't know.

These percentages loosely follow the strength of the different Christian communities in the UK[13], except that the proportion of Catholics is about half what it is for the entire population, and the Baptist and Methodist percentages are four or five times larger.

Other denominations included the United Reformed Church (1%), combinations of denominations (2%), and non-Trinitarian or non-Christian religions of which 1% were Hindus, 1% Muslims, 1% Sikhs, 1% Jews, and then 3 Wiccans, 3 Buddhists, 2 Atheists, 2 Humanists, 2 Jehovah's Witnesses and 2 Rastafarians, which together make up the remaining 1%.

Parents taking their child to church as a baby was more true of Baptists (81%) than Catholics (71%), Pentecostals (71%), Independents (70%), Anglicans (69%), House/New Churches (61%) or Methodists (51%).

The average age of stopping going to church was 9.0 years. Anglicans were slightly less than this (8.9 years), that is, young people left the Church of England earlier than the Roman Catholics (9.6 years), Baptists (9.7 years) or Methodists (9.8 years), but the differences are obviously small. No denomination was keeping their young people significantly longer than others.

Table A4/14 gives the spread of young people by age and by denomination. The New Churches have more aged 10 and 11, the Catholics more aged 12, the Pentecostals aged 13, and the Independents aged 14.

What do Tweenagers like about church?

One question specifically asked young people what they most liked about church by giving them a list to choose from. On average they ticked four things each, but only one factor was agreed by a majority.

51% Opportunity to meet new friends/people

45% Caring people

41% Enjoyable Sunday youth group

34% Enjoyable music

32% Helps me worship God

29% Youth leaders

28% Strong presence of God

28% It is where I have always gone

27% Enjoyable social activities
25% Enjoyable drama
23% Bible teaching
22% Enjoyable mid-week activities
20% Youth worship
19% The minister
13% Not sure.

The first three items and the sixth all related to meeting or interacting with people. Tweenagers love a gang; personal contacts are more important than programmes and structures. Some faith development theorists[14] label the adolescent age as a time of affiliative faith, that is, they need a faith group to which they belong, while others[15] describe this "conforming faith" as "values... to unite one in emotional solidarity with others"[16].

The fourth, fifth and seventh items are all concerned with worship – is this why events like Soul Survivor are increasingly popular? The survey did not ask Tweenagers whether they go to church in the morning or evening, or on Sunday more than mid-week, but the range of answers given suggests any or all may be preferred. But note in the list above Table 6.3 that 49% said they do not go to church on Sunday morning because they don't get up early enough!

A further 7% gave other reasons. These were the sense of belonging (13 responses), the choir (9), the worship (8), time of prayer and peace (6), the food (5), the teaching (5), the activities (4), the fun (4), friends (4), being involved in service (4), going with the family (3) and liking Sunday School/Junior Church (3). There were also four negative comments.

Three of the 15 factors in the above varied with the school grades usually achieved, and three by age. These are illustrated respectively in Figures 6.7 and 6.8.

Generally, as with other questions, the lower the grade the less that particular factor is appreciated. Worshipping God is the exception here. Figure 6.8 suggests that the popularity of youth groups and their leaders peaks about the age of 12.

Figure 6.7: Things liked about church by School Grade usually achieved

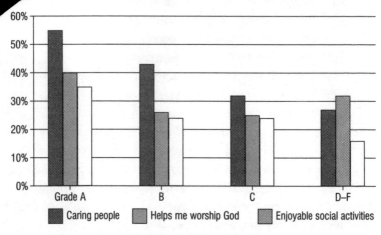

Figure 6.8: Things liked about church by age

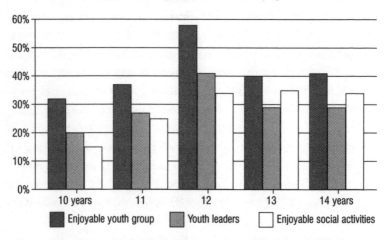

The churchgoing Focus Group were asked similar questions. Fun and friends were very important: "fun things to do" included camps and youth group, while "groups are quite fun with friends". They also cited the desire to "learn a lot of stuff about God". The Scottish Tweenagers were asked separately what they liked about Sunday activities at church for their age group, and about midweek activities. On Sunday they particularly liked the opportunity to learn in a less strict, more relaxed environment where they were doing so alongside their friends and were being taught in a different way from school. Midweek they liked the informality, the fact that they could choose to come rather than be brought by their parents, that they could come with their friends, wear what they like... and eat!

They were also asked what they didn't like about church. Several of the responses were what one might expect: long sermons, songs they didn't know or like, language they didn't understand and services that went on too long. However, they also raised a factor which was considered very important in the Scottish survey: the attitude of the rest of the congregation. They said:

"They are unfriendly people"

"The old people don't like us"

"I don't like the rest of the congregation".

The adult Focus Groups in Scotland were asked to list reasons why they thought 11 to 14 year olds leave the church, and then to vote on the relative importance of these. All three of the Focus Groups with church-based youth workers rated the attitudes of others in the church as either the top or second most important reason why 11 to 14 year olds leave church.

Each group was surprised, with a typical reaction being "I think it is important, but I didn't know other people did". They felt sad, disheartened, angry and worried by the implications, recognising that factors external to the church are often blamed for youngsters leaving, but how they are treated inside the church is at least as important, if not more so.

The Scottish research revealed that:

"11 to 14 year-olds are almost 'non-persons' at church, as being neither children in Sunday School, nor yet really old enough to take an adult role in the 'grown ups' church. Young people don't like being expected to dress smartly or behave properly on a non-school day, being talked down to, being expected to understand language which is full of jargon, or having activities that are scaled down versions of the adults'. In other words, they felt that church is an alien culture for their age group, which they do not like having to fit into."

It was therefore both interesting and worrying to find such responses replicated by the Tweenagers in the English Focus Groups. Ministers and those working with this age group need to consider seriously how they can help older members of the congregation understand and accept Tweenagers as a valid part of the church. It is also vital to provide activities suitable for this age group and teach them in a way they can understand and accept.

Taking part in activities

Six typical activities for churchgoing Tweenagers were suggested, and each asked how frequently they did them. Answers were as follows where the positive answers have been made to add to 100%:

Table 6.9: Frequency of certain Tweenagers' activities

Activity	NO, I never do this %	Daily %	Weekly %	Monthly %	Sometimes[17] %	Avrge times a year
Pray to God	26	43	19	5	33	168
Read part of the Bible	38	15	29	6	50	72
Attend church-based youth group	48	4	71	8	17	53
Take a part in church services	48	4	23	19	54	30
Attend a Bible Study Group	80	10	45	10	35	62
Lead a church based youth group	89	9	27	9	55	49

Praying was the most frequent of these activities, with those who did pray doing so on average every other day. Three-fifths of Tweenagers said they read the Bible, usually about once every five days. Half attended a church-based youth group or took an active part in services, the first weekly, the second once a fortnight on average.

Few attended a Bible Study Group and even fewer led a youth group, but those that did either, did so about once a week.

All these activities, except attending a Bible Study Group, varied by the grades normally achieved at school. Table A4/16 in Appendix 4 gives the details with frequency expressed as average times a year for those undertaking an activity. This shows, as with other results, that those with the higher grades are more likely to undertake a particular activity, and among those doing the activity those with higher grades are likely to do them more frequently.

Likewise two factors varied significantly by age, and the figures are given in Table A4/18. This shows that as young people get older they were less likely to undertake a particular activity, and the older ones still doing the activity did it less often.

The figures naturally varied by whether the Tweenager was a Christian or not: there was a progressive decline in undertaking activities, from being a Christian to being unsure, to no longer being a Christian and not being a Christian, and a decreasing frequency with which any activities were undertaken. Details are in Table A4/17. Those belonging to other religions took part in activities at about the same rate as those unsure or not a Christian, but when they did take part in an activity it was as often or more often than Christians did!

This survey suggests that rather more Tweenagers read their Bible than a more extensive survey carried out by Professor Leslie Francis on a large sample of pupils aged 13 and 14[18]. Two-thirds, 66%, of his sample never read the Bible, though of those who did, 15%, the same percentage as in the RAKES survey, read it every day. He found that age, gender (for less frequent readers), social class, church attendance and denomination all made a significant difference to Bible reading[19]. We have found that age and gender did not make a large difference, but being a Christian and the grade usually achieved at school did. We did not measure it by social class, although standard of school work may be, at least partly, a proxy for social class.

Another survey among 13 to 15 year olds by Leslie Francis found that "Bible reading makes a small but significant contribution to promoting a negative attitude toward drug use among this age group."[20]

Would you tell your friends if you went to church?

Half the respondents, 48%, replied YES to this question. A third, 32%, replied MAYBE, and the remaining fifth, 20%, said NO. Girls were more likely to tell their friends than boys (53% to 43%). The 48% who would say Yes was made up of 60% of those who were Christians, and 37% of those who weren't sure, and 27% each for those no longer a Christian or not a Christian.

Some might feel that the 60% for Christians should be nearer 100% – aren't all Christians supposed to witness to their faith? One pair of parents, John and Sue Ritter, strongly urge other parents not to add to the pressures on their children by such expectations[21]. Some Tweenagers feel guilty about not witnessing to their school mates, but the Ritters point out that parents need to encourage their children, so that they will talk about their faith naturally and at the right moment as the opportunity affords.

Those with the higher grades would be more likely to say YES – 56% of those normally getting grade A, 43% grade B, 41% grade C and 36% of those with lower grades.

These percentages varied by age as shown in Figure 6.10. Younger and older children were more inclined to tell their friends they went to church, but once firmly ensconced in secondary school, more became defensive and would not tell them. Uncertainty ("maybe") was greatest in the year of transition, when aged 11, perhaps because new friendships are being established and children are not yet sure how much they can share in the new relationships.

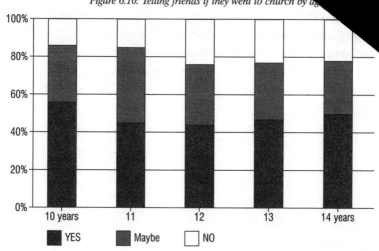

Figure 6.10: Telling friends if they went to church by age

What would your friends say?

One question asked, "What do you think your friends and other people would say if they thought that you went to a church or a youth activity based in a church?" Five answers were suggested plus an open alternative. They replied:

- 33% I have already told my friends that I go
- 32% They might make fun of me or think I am stupid or uncool
- 16% They might be curious and ask me questions
- 6% I would be too shy to tell anyone
- 3% They belong to another religion so they would not be bothered
- 10% answered in other ways.

Other answers varied from "they wouldn't care" and "they'd be proud of me" to "they'd beat me up" and "they would be curious" (the last being the most common answer).

These answers varied by whether or not a Tweenager was Christian. Details are given in Table A4/19, and indicate that a quart-

not Christian are more likely to think their
, and that over half, 52%, of those no longer
nds would make fun of them. Could this lat-
ons why they are no longer Christian?

127

how once again these answers varied by the
gra   usually get at school. Table 6.11 gives details:

*Table 6.11: Expected response to admission to churchgoing
by the grades Tweenagers normally achieved*

Reaction	Mostly As %	Mostly Bs %	Mostly Cs %	Mostly D-Fs %	*Overall* %
I have already told my friends I go	41	29	21	28	33
They might make fun of me	26	34	43	43	32
They might ask me questions	14	17	20	23	16
I would be too shy to tell anyone	5	6	5	8	6
They belong to another religion	2	4	2	4	3
Other reactions	12	10	9	4	10

Those with higher grades are more likely to have already told
their friends they go to church. They also felt they were less likely to
be made fun of (because they were known to be good academically?),
and fewer thought their friends would be curious (because they
expected they might go to church?).

Likewise the answers varied by age. Details are given in Table
A4/20 in Appendix 4. This shows that those in the middle years, 11,
12 and 13, would be those least likely to tell their friends they went
church, and that, generally, as children got older the more they
thought they would be made fun of or thought stupid or uncool.

Girls were more likely to have already told their friends (39%
to 26% boys), but boys were more likely to think that their friends
would make fun of them (37% to 27%) or be curious (19% to 14%).

Answers also varied by how Tweenagers described their home.
The detail is given in Table A4/21, but shows:

- Those who feel secure and loved at home, and those homes where "each of us is trying to love each other", are both more likely to have told their friends they go to church and are less likely to think they might be made fun of.
- Homes where Tweenagers "sometimes feel loved and other times don't" and where they "usually feel uncomfortable and would rather be elsewhere" are both less likely to have told their friends they go to church and are more likely to think they might be made fun of.
- Those living in homes where they feel comfortable but acknowledge they are not a close, loving family are much less likely to have told their friends they go to church and are much more likely to think they might be made fun of.

In other words, home circumstances are very important when sharing with their friends about churchgoing habits (and perhaps about other items which might be regarded as personal?).

Those who think their friends may be curious, or who feel too shy to tell or whose friends belong to other religions do not vary significantly by age, gender, school grade or home circumstances. It is only having told friends, or fear of being made fun of that are the age-sensitive questions.

Changing the church

Both Focus Groups were asked how the church needs to change to make it more attractive to people their age. The non-churchgoers' answers show how alien the experience of church is for them:

"Change the inside of the buildings",

"Add some laughs" or "Have a 'Happy Week'"

"Sing songs like Sister Act"

"Use ordinary words"

"Make the services shorter"

"Make them smell better"

"Include more young people in the services".

Some of the churchgoers' answers were similar:

"Have more understandable, simpler sermons"

"Make the talks / sermons shorter" "and more exciting".

(When asked what length sermon or talk they would like, the response was 5 to 10 minutes.)

"Make the service shorter"

(Half an hour was considered about the right length.)

However, some of the responses showed their desire that church should "work" for them:

"The songs are mostly '80s stuff, not what we like"

"There should be special services for us, not just for older teenagers"

"They could be more friendly, what about coffee and food in the service?"

"Why can't a younger person do the sermon sometimes?"

"There should be more active sermons" to which another added,

"The whole service should be more active".

These Tweenagers were not complaining about the Christian faith, it was the church they found it difficult to relate to.

What are the challenges?

"He is 14. Six years ago his parents' marriage broke up. The father left town and did not keep in touch. The mother remarried, and the relationship between the boy and his stepfather has not been the best. 'You are good for nothing' is the frequent, angry judgement of the stepfather. The mother can't do much. She tries to be less harsh on her teenage son but feels constrained to accept her husband's views. The son is puzzled. He feels he is not wanted at home. He recognizes that no one really loves him or cares about him. He feels he must leave home. But before he does that, he comes to see you, his pastor. What do you say to him?"[22]

Such was the challenge in one article. It may not be the out-working of a broken family, but drunkenness, drugs, or pornography which could be the subject of such a query. In the UK today there are perhaps 8,000 youth workers, roughly one for every six churches (although perhaps half this figure are Anglican curates or Free Church Assistant Ministers). It may well be that they, rather than the pastor, are faced with such pastoral problems.

In the Anglican Diocese of Salisbury, a Youth Forum Day was held in October 2000. One of the outcomes was a list of the top ten problems in children's and youth work. The item at the top of the list was "Need for inspired youth workers", perhaps to help with problems such as those just described, or to confront the challenge of relationships with such damaged young people. The other nine were:

- The changing nature of Sunday and the clash of priorities, especially for families
- The church and Church Council do not always support children's work; some adults seem to deliberately put them off!
- Not being open-minded about who can work with young people
- Needing to have enough young people to form a "gang"
- Holding a youth group across several churches
- There is a very large generation gap
- The changing nature of education, including the internet
- The challenge of holiday clubs to reach non-church young people
- The challenge of youth worship, and the success of churches with special youth services.

Youth services

In 1998 14% of churches in England said they held a youth service once a month[23]. While some probably would otherwise be called Family Services or All-age Services, others would be services run both for young people and by young people. A survey of member churches of the Evangelical Alliance in 1997 showed that 26% had a "youth church".[24] A different detailed analysis[25] showed that holding such services was a key reason why some churches grew in the 1990s.

Part of the reason for that growth was not just that youth were encouraged to do their own thing. The church leadership had to take a risk in allowing them to do that. These youth services are different! From personal experience I can testify that the music is loud, rather different from that usually played in church[26], and that the programme is fast moving, varied and informal. It is also joyful, lively and challenging!

Such services began to achieve publicity through the Nine O'Clock Service held in the late 1980s in St Thomas Church, Crookes, Sheffield, although it quickly grew too large for the church and moved to other premises. It regularly attracted congregations of 500 and was warmly welcomed by the Church of England, with the Archbishop of Canterbury saying he'd like to see one such in every Diocese[27]. This particular service received unwanted publicity because of leadership breach of trust, but a wide range of similar events have since developed in many places.

Much has been learned from such initial experiments, often with older young people. Today, Tweenagers help to lead worship experiences regularly in Soul Survivor in Watford, or as The Warehouse, part of the Pioneer stream of New Churches in Chichester.

Youth services usually attract those of 15 or above, and while the attendance range and ages are not known definitively are probably mostly young people aged 18 to 25. Some, like the St Thomas Mass held in Helsinki, Finland once a month, have run for years, but those attending it enjoyed it so much that they didn't leave when they reached 25 or 30. They have thus grown older with the Mass, which should perhaps now be called the "Thirties St Thomas Mass"! Why have they stayed? A survey[28] showed that after the music the second most important characteristic of a church needs to be "a place to get closer to people and to be loved", indicated by 25% of those under 25. This particular congregation gives that.

Another survey, this time of 10,000 teenagers, undertaken in 2000 in the United States by the Navigators found similarly that a factor of key importance for their involvement in church was a "welcoming atmosphere where you can be yourself"[29].

Although this report primarily focuses on the 10 to 14 age-group, these services are mentioned here because if they are successful for older teenagers, could something like them work for Tweenagers as those in the Focus Group suggested? Some resources for such do exist.[30] Youth services are often organised with the help of a church's Youth Worker, and tend to be held in larger churches[31].

Sunday School

Some Sunday Schools work brilliantly. Although only 4%[32] of the nation's children attended them in 2000, there are a few which are highly successful. Taking its model after the Metro Church Sunday School in Brooklyn, New York (which 20,000 children attend), a similar project in Liverpool attracts over 700 children and one church in Sunderland visits more than 90 families a week.

The secret behind these Sunday Schools is the small army of volunteers who visit the children every week. "These personal visits place people in someone else's world, and provide a person-to-person relationship. Personal visits prevent alienation, prepare young personalities for spiritual challenge, and promote productivity. They project an image."[33]

In the children's story by Margery Williams[34], *The Velveteen Rabbit,* an old skin horse that had been in the toy box for many years talks to a newcomer stuffed rabbit about being real. "What is real?" asks the rabbit one day. "Does it mean having things that buzz inside you and a stick-out handle?"

"Real isn't how you are made," replies the old horse. "It's a thing that happens to you. You see, when a child loves you for a long, long time, not just to play with, but really loves you, then you become real. It does not happen all at once. It usually takes a long time. By the time you are real, most of your hair has been loved off, your eyes drop out, you get loose in the joints and very shabby. But these things don't really matter at all, because once you are real you can't be ugly except to the people who don't understand."

"That conversation, as fictitious as it might be, actually reflects the reality being sought by folks today," wrote Bill Wilson, director of the Metro Church Sunday School[35]. It reflects also the earlier comments made of older teenagers about the St Thomas Mass in Helsinki.

So what does all this mean?

This chapter has shown:
- Those with highest school grades (normally getting As) are almost twice as likely to be regular churchgoers as those getting lower grades.
- Those *not going* to church don't go because they think it is boring, not cool, and, frankly, can't be bothered. Although these answers were measured against Tweenagers, they are identical to those found for older teenagers. All three reasons become more important with increasing age.
- Subsidiary reasons included not being able to get up early enough (suggesting the importance of Tweenage activities later on on Sundays or midweek) and that their parents didn't encourage them.
- While parents are naturally a huge influence in the lives of their children, the importance of grandparents and their example also emerges here, as in previous chapters.
- There is a large amount of ignorance as to what exactly church is about; hence the importance of clergy and other visits to local schools. Likewise it is important for churches to welcome visits by schools "preferably with the heating on, so that it feels nice![36]
- Tweenagers tended to stop going to church in their 11th year – the year most move to secondary school. In general terms those who stop have been going for four years, longer if they started before they were 5, and much less if they started when 8 or 9. "Stoppers" didn't enjoy church, and felt they had grown out of it.

- This shows the importance of having good teaching for those aged 7 to 10 years of age. These years lay the foundation of a child's long-term reactions to church (and maybe Christianity).
- Tweenagers going only occasionally to church either go for the Occasional Offices, or at the main Festivals, or on other special occasions.
- Two-thirds of Tweenagers currently attending church regularly started going because their parents took them. They went to learn about God and Jesus and because they enjoyed it. Those no longer Christian assumed those who did go went because they'd always gone and because their parents made them.
- Denomination of church attended made little difference to attitudes towards church or length of time a Tweenager stayed.
- Churchgoing Tweenagers enjoyed church because of the people they met there – new people, caring people, their peers. The higher the school grade they usually obtained the more important these were.
- Three-quarters of Tweenagers said they prayed and two-thirds said they read parts of the Bible. Those with higher school grades did more Christian activities, as naturally did those who were Christian.
- Tweenagers are not against the Christian faith, it is the church they find difficulty relating to. What they experience there is so alien to their lifestyle that non-churchgoing Tweenagers do not understand it and churchgoers want to change it radically.
- Churchgoing Tweenagers feel unwanted by older members of the congregation. The attitudes of older churchgoers was felt by church youth workers in Scotland to be one of the main reasons this age group leave church.
- Half of the respondents would tell their friends that they went to church, especially those achieving higher school grades. But a third felt that their friends would make fun of them if they said they went to church, especially boys and those getting lower grades. The security they felt at home was, however, also a crucial element in whether they felt confident enough to say they went to church.

- Leaders face tough challenges to meet these issues, and the personal circumstances of Tweenagers in a pastoral context.
- About one church in 14 holds some form of regular youth service, some of which are very popular, especially if led by young people themselves.
- The huge Metro Church Sunday School in Brooklyn, repeated here in Liverpool and elsewhere, shows that activities for this age group can be made very attractive. The example of regularly visiting their homes, if volunteers can be found, is one way of helping to form strong relationships.

NOTES

[1] The statistical correlation, however, although significant at –0.09, is weak. The gender correlation is also weak, at +0.09. 181 respondents did not give their usual school grade; 62% of these were regular churchgoers.

[2] *Reaching and Keeping Teenagers,* Peter Brierley, MARC, Tunbridge Wells, 1993, Table 41, Page 134.

[3] Personal email from Richard Bromley, based on his own Tweenager research in 2001.

[4] Survey reported in article in the *Church of England Newspaper,* 20 October 2000, Page 4.

[5] *Church of Scotland: Ministry among Young People* – Focus Groups, Heather Wraight, for the Parish Education Department, Church of Scotland, Christian Research, London, 2000.

[6] At least one other study puts the major year of exodus a year or two later – the findings of those attending Anglican churches in Deanery of Erith, Diocese of Rochester, Congregational Attitudes and Beliefs Survey, Christian Research, 2001.

[7] *The Tide is Running Out,* Peter Brierley, Christian Research, London, 2000, Figure 35, Page 169.

[8] See *Touching the Future,* Rev Gill Dallow, The Bible Reading Fellowship, Oxford, 2002.

[9] Described later.

[10] *Steps to the Future,* Peter Brierley, Scripture Union, Bletchley, and Christian Research, London, 2000, Page 68, where the percentage is 56%.

[11] Reported on their website, www.adventist.org/news/data/2000 on 9 May 2001, on publication of the book *Why Our Teenagers Leave the Church,* published by the Review and Herald Publishing Association, Dudley, United States.

[12] Op. cit., (Footnote 2) Table 39, Page 131.

[13] As given, for example, in *Religious Trends* No 3, 2002/2003, Table 2.3.1.

[14] Such as John Westerhoff.

[15] Such as Professor James Fowler, Center for Research in Faith and Moral Development, Emory University, Atlanta, Georgia, United States.

[16] Op. cit., (Footnote 2) Page 159.

[17] Taken as twice a year.

[18] Article "Who reads the Bible? A study of 13–15 year olds" by Professor Leslie J Francis in the *British Journal of Religious Education*, Volume 3, Number 22, 2000, Page 165.

[19] This study is illustrated in *Religious Trends* No 3, 2002/2003, Christian Research, Page 6.4.

[20] "The relationship between Bible reading and attitude toward substance use among 13–15 year olds", Professor Leslie Francis, University of Wales, Bangor in *Religious Education*, Volume 97, Number 1, Winter 2002, Page 44.

[21] *The Brat Pack*, 11–14 year olds, how do you treat yours?, John and Sue Ritter, Marshall Pickering, London, 1994, Page 115.

[22] Article "Youth in trouble: what can pastors do?" in *Ministry*, International Journal for Pastors, General Conference of Seventh-Day Adventists, Hagerstown, Maryland, United States, March 1997, Page 14.

[23] Op. cit., (Footnote 7) Page 162.

[24] Evangelical Alliance Survey, reported in *Church Growth Digest*, Year 19, Issue 1, Autumn 1997, Page 5.

[25] *Church Growth in the 1990s*, Dr Peter Brierley, Research report, Springboard and Christian Research, 2000.

[26] At least one research study however has shown that teenagers believe that the kind of music which is "right for a church" is choral music, not instrumental, sung by a group of singers rather than a soloist, and characterised by a simple musical texture and understandable text. Report "Teenagers and Church Music", 1995 research by Dr Barbara Resch of 479 American teenagers, reported on website: www.worship.lcms.org/insert/churchmusic, 5 September 2001.

[27] Article "Youth Churches – the Future or Failure of the Church?" by Simon Hall in *Church Growth Digest*, Year 19, Issue 1, Autumn 1997, Page 8.

[28] *In Every Place, both high and low*, A survey of Finland's spiritual state and the possibilities of church growth, Heikki Lassila et al, DAWN Finland, 1995, and quoted in *Quadrant*, Christian Research, January 1997, Page 3.

[29] Article "The cool church" by Rick Lawrence in the magazine *Group*, 6th May, 2001, Page 37, with details on the Navigator Press website: www.navpress.com/ctt

[30] Such as *CPAS DIY Celebrations* and *Search Engine, Young Sarum*, the Newsletter for people working with children and youth in Salisbury Diocese, email: salsdbejo@aol.com, or the magazine *Together with Children*, published by the National Society for Promoting Religious Education, in association with the Board of Education of the General Synod of the Church of England, website: www.togetherwithchildren.co.uk

[31] The same Evangelical Alliance Survey showed that of the 1,000 responding churches, 40% of those with a congregation of 200+ had a Youth Worker in 1997, compared with 13% of those with between 100 and 199, 7% of those with between 70 and 99, and 2% of smaller churches. 44% of churches with a congregation over 200 had a Youth Church, 34% of those between 100 and 199 of 200+, 25% of those between 70 and 99, 20% of those between 40 and 60, and 13% of smaller churches.

[32] *Religious Trends* No 2, 2000/2001, HarperCollins and Christian Research, London, Page 2.15.

[33] Article "Entering a Child's World" by Bill Wilson, *Renewal,* Number 285, February 2000, Page 30.

[34] First published by Heinemann, London, 1922. In 1991 edition, Page 5.

[35] Op. cit., (Footnote 33).

[36] Martin Robinson, formerly of the Bible Society, mentions one visit when the church was so cold that it gave totally the wrong image to the Tweenagers looking round!

Honesty and other personal values

Mark's teacher was on the phone to his mother. "Mrs Smith, your son did something in class that surprised me so much that I thought you should know about it immediately." The mother grew worried. Her 10 year old son was usually well-behaved.

"Nothing like this has happened in all my years of teaching," the woman continued. "This morning I was teaching a lesson on creative writing. And, as I always do, I told the story of the ant and the grasshopper." She recounted the story as she had in class:

"The ant works hard all summer and stores up plenty of food. But the grasshopper plays all summer and does no work. Then winter comes. The grasshopper begins to starve because he has no food. So he begins to beg, 'Please, Mr Ant, you have much food. Please let me eat, too.' Then I said, 'Boys and girls, your job is to write the ending of the story.'

"Your son, Mark, raised his hand. 'Miss, may I draw a picture?'

"I said, 'Well, yes, Mark, if you like, you may draw a picture. But first you must write the ending to the story.'

"As in all the years past, most of the students said the ant shared his food through the winter and both the ant and the grasshopper lived. A few children wrote, "No, Mr Grasshoppper. You should have worked in the summer. Now, I have just enough food for myself." So the ant lived and the grasshopper died.'

"But your son ended the story in a way different from any other child, ever. He wrote, 'So the ant gave all his food to the grasshopper. The grasshopper lived through the winter, but the ant died.'

"And the picture? At the bottom, Mark had drawn three crosses."[1]

Living with myself

Some of the early questions on the form touched on general behavioural principles. This chapter does not especially look at sexual morality which was considered in the fifth chapter "Friends and Leisure Activities".

"Cheating was a regular, accepted activity in my school... No one ever questioned it or reported it," said Karen[2]. How far were such attitudes generally true? A range of statements were made all relating to how a Tweenager might react or behave, and they were asked to indicate whether they agreed or disagreed with each one or simply felt neutral. Table 7.1 gives their answers in order of what they agreed about:

Table 7.1: Tweenagers' agreement with various moral statements

Statement	Agree %	Not sure %	Disagree %
Stealing is always wrong	73	15	12
It is always wrong to cheat	67	19	14
Sometimes it is necessary to tell a lie	66	21	13
The main purpose in life is enjoyment and personal fulfilment	55	30	15
Life's too short to worry	43	28	29
It is always wrong to tell lies	42	28	30
It is better to get even than mad	38	36	26
In times of trouble or crisis I feel all alone	36	28	36
Everyone needs a hero in their life	29	41	30
There is no one I consider my hero or role model	28	31	41
My opinions and attitudes are not taken seriously	27	42	31
The future will be better than today	25	61	14
It's OK to copy things from others if you're in a hurry	24	31	45
One cannot really make a difference in this world	22	23	55
It is OK to take little things like pencils from school	12	17	71

There are four statements which command a majority – two which outright support honesty, but a third which shows a contrasting (but remarkably pragmatic) attitude that sometimes lies have to be used! A majority also believe that life is for enjoyment and fulfilment.

The mass of comments in between are accepted by less than half, but more than a fifth, between 20% and 50%. Only one is outside these limits, again an issue of honesty with nearly three-quarters, 71%, disagreeing that it is OK to take things like pencils from school. Honesty of action therefore emerges as a central value of Tweenagers from the evidence of this question, a value which, however, may not extend into speech (only two-fifths, 42%, agreed it was always wrong to tell lies, and over a quarter, 28%, were uncertain).

Just as a majority felt it was wrong to cheat so a majority disagreed that copying from others was permissible if you were in a hurry. These two answers are at least consistent. Young women rather than young men felt this way (73% to 61%), the only one of these statements where gender made a difference.

Some of the statements varied by school year. The detail is given in Table A4/22 in Appendix 4, and it is immediately apparent that honesty is a value that wanes as Tweenagers get older. Ten year olds are far more idealistic in this regard than those who are 14! Furthermore, it was only the issues of honesty that varied by age – for the others they agreed across the full age-range. So honesty is an ideal which becomes eroded as Tweenagers grow older.

Honesty was more important for Tweenagers who went to church regularly. Details are given in Table A4/23. This finding is exhaustively confirmed by the work of the Michael Ramsey Professor of Applied Theology at the University of Kent at Canterbury, Dr Robin Gill[3]. Those who have stopped going to church are more likely to disagree on a variety of issues than those who have never been to church, a kind of perverse spirituality that has been observed elsewhere – those returning to church were found to be less spiritual in their attitudes than those who had never left[4]. There were two statements which varied by denomination – sometimes telling a lie and life being mainly for enjoyment and personal fulfilment – which those who were Catholics and Methodists both supported more strongly than other denominations, perhaps because that's the way they generally talk about life. (See Table A4/24).

However, honesty did not generally vary by the grades that a Tweenager usually obtained. Instead the grade As were usually less likely to agree other particular statements than those usually getting grade Cs or lower. Details are given in Table A4/25. Thus 33% of grade As felt it was better to get even than mad, compared with 47% of grade Cs. A fifth, 21%, of grade As felt it was OK to copy things from other people if you were in a hurry, while half of those agreeing, 44%, were grade D–Fs. Thus the grading usually obtained was relevant in determining some of a person's individual attitudes and values, with those getting lower grades likely to take perhaps less traditional views.

This question showed that of the various values tested in the statements, those relating to honesty were the ones which varied most by age and church attendance. Those relating to attitude and the future varied most by grades usually achieved. As author Leonard Sweet remarks, "They care deeply for integrity. And what gives anything integrity is not a state of perfection but a story that proves its authenticity."[5]

Helping others

"Do you do any activity that helps other people around where you live?" was a short question to which two-fifths, 38%, answered NO and the remaining three-fifths, 62%, therefore answered YES. How Tweenagers did what they did varied, with every other respondent giving two ways. The main methods were:

- 33% through my school
- 22% on my own
- 19% through my church, and
- 18% through other groups like Scouts or Guides.

Helping others through their school declined with age as Figure 7.2 indicates, although there was a slight increase with the very oldest children.

Figure 7.2: Helping others through school by age

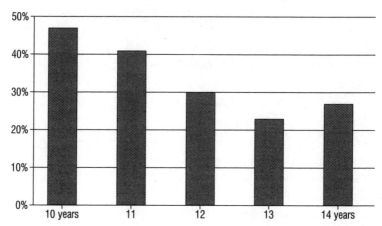

Helping others varied with church attendance. Those who went regularly were most likely to help others; those who went occasionally were likely to help others more than those who had given up going or who never went. Again this supports Robin Gill's thesis. Details are in Table A4/26[6].

Money on the pavement

If a Tweenager found a £20 note on the pavement what would they do? Would it be any different if they found two £50 notes? We gave them a choice, and their answers are reflected in Figure 7.3.

While a small proportion of Tweenagers, 10%, would be uncertain whether to leave the money or pick up one £50 note and leave the other, and a few more would give the money to charity (13% for the £20 note, 8% for the £100), the majority would choose between keeping it (58% for the £20 note, 40% for the £100) or handing it in to the police station (24% for the £20 note, 42% for the £100). Thus more than twice as many would keep the £20 note as hand it in, whereas slightly more would hand in the £100 than keep it.

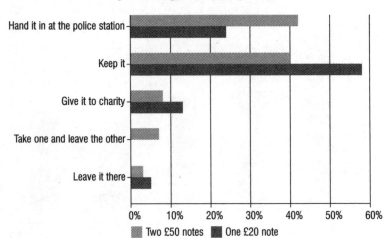

Figure 7.3: Responses to finding money

Things have changed since the mid-1990s! When an identical question was posed to 2,000 adults in 1995[7], the majority were in favour of handing in both sums of money to the police (55% for £20 and 80% for £100), though rather more would have kept the £20 than the £100 (22% to 8%). There is an age difference of course but a majority of 21st century Tweenagers would keep £20 if they found it, and two-fifths £100, but a quarter would be honest enough to hand in £20 and two-fifths £100 to a police station.

These figures varied quite considerably by age, however[8]. As Tweenagers get older they are much more likely to keep the £20 (almost twice the proportion of 14 year olds than 10 year olds) and less likely to hand it to the police. But while similar trends are observable for the £100 they are much more muted. Tweenagers may know what to do with £20 but are less certain with £100 – though at 12 years of age more will keep the money than hand it in. The detailed figures are in Table 7.4.

Table 7.4: Responses to finding money by age

Finding one £20 note	10 %	11 %	12 %	13 %	14 %	Overall %
Leave it there	6	5	5	4	6	5
Give to charity	21	15	13	8	9	13
Keep it	39	50	61	71	68	58
Hand it in to the police	34	30	21	17	17	24

Finding two £50 notes	10 %	11 %	12 %	13 %	14 %	Overall %
Leave it or there	13	10	11	8	8	10
Give to charity	11	8	8	6	8	8
Keep it	31	33	43	47	46	40
Hand in to police	45	49	38	39	38	42

Boys were much more likely to keep the money than girls whether they found £20 or £100. Likewise those who normally achieved grade C–Fs were much more likely to keep the money than those getting grade As, whether they found £20 or £100, with grade Bs somewhere in between. Honesty (if this is what these answers are measuring) is more prevalent among girls and those getting higher grades. Details are in Table A4/27.

Reactions to finding money varied also by whether or not Tweenagers went to church regularly. Those who did were much more likely to hand in the money to the police (35% for £20, 58% for £100) than those who never went to church (12% for £20 and 23% for £100), again confirming Robin Gill's thesis. This and similar results show the gulf in thinking and probably culture between those involved with the church and those who are not. Those who attend church occasionally and those who have stopped going are between the two extremes. Table A4/28 gives the relevant percentages.

Table A4/29 gives a further analysis, this time by internet usage. It shows that the more Tweenagers use the internet the less likely they are to hand any money they find to the police and the more they are likely to keep it. This is true both for finding £20 and £100.

This question has been analysed by a number of different factors. If we just look at the one answer "Keep it" then the variations seen above and in Appendix 4 may be summarised as in Table 7.5:

Table 7.5: Keeping money by different factors

Factor	Range	Keeping £20 %	+/-	Keeping £100 %	+/-
Age	10 years	39%	} 29%	31%	} 15%
	14 years	68%		46%	
Gender	Female	51%	} 16%	32%	} 18%
	Male	67%		50%	
Internet usage	Up to once a month	50%	} 21%	32%	} 28%
	More than daily	71%		60%	
Grades usually	Mostly As	51%	} 21%	32%	} 29%
obtained	Mostly C–Fs	72%		61%	
Frequency of	Regular	40%	} 37%	24%	} 36%
churchgoing	Never	77%		60%	
Overall		58%	—	40%	—

Table 7.5 tells several things:

- Fewer Tweenagers will keep £100 than £20 if found on the pavement.
- Tweenagers who are older; male; usually get grades C–F; use the internet more than once a day; and the non-churchgoing are all more likely to keep any money they find than others.
- The differences between keeping £20 or £100 are mostly smaller than that between the characteristics themselves. In other words, the characteristics are more important discriminatory variables than the amount of money (apart from age).
- Of these five factors, that relating to church attendance is the one that produces the greatest differences.
- The second factor, however, varies between age for finding £20 and grades usually obtained for £100, with internet usage close behind.

Insofar as answers to this question reveal innate honesty, regular church attendance is the likely best mechanism for encouraging or demonstrating it. This is an important finding which, while supporting Robin Gill's finding that churchgoing enculturates values, goes further by demonstrating that other variables which might be expected to be more important (such as age, gender and ability) are not.

Things one shouldn't have done

There are a number of actions which Tweenagers (those aged 10 to 14 here) are not allowed to do because of their age, others that are generally frowned on, some that are illegal for everyone (whatever their ages) and family or physical matters that are best avoided. We selected 11 of these, none of them related overtly to sexuality, and asked how many Tweeenagers had done any of them in the past three months. Answers fell into two groups. There were those which about half or more of the Tweenagers had done, and those actions undertaken by a small but significant minority. In the first group there were three actions:

- 69% had watched a horror or violent film
- 56% had lied to a parent, teacher or other adult
- 46% had lied to a friend or another young person

That so many have watched a horror or violent film is no surprise if 98% of Tweenagers watch television in their spare time, and 61% have a TV set in their bedroom, and 36% a video player[9]. When asked what type of programme they watched, 81% said comedy and 79% said films, the top two categories. So what these answers indicate is that many Tweenagers watch films which their parents, or teachers, might not wish them to. Boys are more likely than girls to watch horror and violent films – 76% to 66%, the only one of these 11 characteristics to vary by gender.

If 66% of Tweenagers agree that it is sometimes necessary to tell a lie (Table 7.1), it is not perhaps surprising that in the previous three months half of them had done so. Their answers suggest they lie slightly more to adults than to their peers, but there isn't much difference! This probably reflects the declining respect for authority in society generally in that authority figures are not treated significantly better than their peers.

The behaviours of the significant minorities (these items are not necessarily answered by the same Tweenagers) were:

- 20% consumed enough alcohol to get drunk
- 20% intentionally tried to hurt someone's feelings
- 17% intentionally tried to hurt someone physically
- 15% cheated on an exam or test
- 13% smoked cigarettes
- 7% stolen money
- 6% used an illegal drug
- 5% had shoplifted.

Some of these activities varied with age. Table A4/30 gives details. Three-fifths, 59%, of those aged ten watched horror films, a percentage which gradually rose to nearly four-fifths, 77% by age 14. Lying to adults increased also with age, from 41% at 10 to 67% at 14. Other items are reflected in Figure 7.6:

Figure 7.6: Certain activities by age

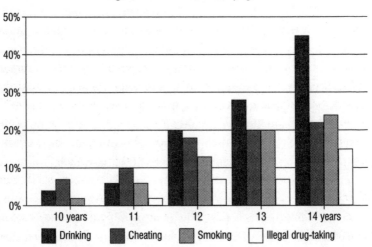

These results are generally typical of other studies and are similar to government figures. For example, the Department of Health in 1998 found that 7% of 13 year olds, 17% of 14 year olds and 25% of 15 year olds were regular cigarette smokers[10]. Girls are more likely to smoke than boys, and in 1996 13% of those aged 11 to 15 were regular cigarette smokers, a percentage which had fallen slightly to 10% by 2000[11]. The government want to see the percentage below 9% by 2010. Perhaps many are similar to Prince William who "tried smoking but didn't like it"[12]! "Telling kids about the risk of lung disease is unlikely to dissuade them. Instead, appeal to issues that concern youngsters. Talk about bad breath and stained teeth."[13]

The Department of Health also found that 54% of 16 year olds drank alcohol, men an average of six units a week, and women 4.5.[14] A European School Survey in 1999 found that 29% of 15 to 16 year olds in the UK said they had already been drunk twenty or more times[15]. A Joseph Rowntree Report evaluating the activities of 14,000 young people found that "binge drinking is commonplace among children as young as 13... a quarter of pupils aged 13 and 14 claimed to have downed five or more alcoholic drinks in a single session."[16]

A Home Office study found 45% of those aged 16 to 19 had taken at least one illegal drug[17]; it is not inconsistent that in this study 15% of those aged 14 have tried an illegal drug. Another study showed that 11% of those aged 11 to 15 in 1998 and 14% in 1999 had experimented with drugs in the past year[18]. "By far the most common illegal drug used by this age group was cannabis; 11% reported using this in the previous year; 1% said they had used crack or cocaine"[19] emerged from another official report[20]. The RAKES forms were anonymous, but these kinds of confirmation suggest that respondents were reasonably honest in answering this question.

Behaviour is also linked to the grades a Tweenager usually gets at school. Those getting mostly As are more likely to be law-abiding than those getting grades C to F, with grade B people somewhere in between. Table A4/31 gives the detail.

Behaviour also varies by whether Tweenagers go to church. As with previous questions, regular churchgoers indulge in these activities less than those who never go to church, but lest it be thought that all churchgoing Tweenagers are "goody-goodies", it should be noted from Table A4/32 that of regular Tweenager church-goers:

- Over half, 51% have watched a horror film in the last three months (against 85% watching one who never go to church)
- 14% (one in seven) have intentionally tried to hurt someone physically (against 25%)
- 8% have drunk enough to get drunk (against 31%)
- 6% have smoked a cigarette (against 20%)
- 3% have stolen money (against 12%)
- 2% have been shoplifting (against 8%) and
- 1% have used an illegal drug (against 11%).

Regular churchgoing Tweenagers are therefore far from immune to the lure of peer pressure. This reinforces the importance of talking about such subjects as drugs, drinking, smoking, stealing, etc. at youth club or similar organisation. The percentage using drugs in this study is less than the 10% found among young people aged 12 to 16 by those attending Spring Harvest in 1995[21].

There was one interesting result of Tweenagers who admitted drinking enough in the last three months to get drunk. On average 20%, this varied from those who were Church of England at 55%, Catholic 10%, Methodist 8%, Baptist 3%, Pentecostals 2%, New Church 1% and others at 21%!

Of those who would be honest enough to tell their friends if they went to church or a church-based activity, only 15% had drunk too much in the past three months, but of those who wouldn't tell their friends they went to church, 35% had drunk too much. An unequivocal church commitment seems, therefore, to have a signifi-cant impact on marginal behaviour.

Sources of values

A 'slideometer' was used in the Focus Groups, with the Tweenagers being asked to rate different possible sources of values, and decide their relative importance. They came up with the following scores (out of 10, with 10 as the high value), which are here compared with scores in an identical exercise in the Gen X Focus Groups (in decreasing order for non-churchgoers aged 10 to 14):

Table 7.7: Different groups' rating of sources of values

Value	Churchgoers		Non-churchgoers	
	10–14s	*Gen X*	*10–14s*	*Gen X*
Family	9.0	8.5	9.5	7.0
Friends	8.0	4.0	9.0	6.5
Teachers	5.0	1.5	8.0	5.0
Church	8.0	9.0	7.5	4.0
Media	2.0	0.5	6.0	7.0
Partner/Spouse	—	7.0	—	6.0

It can be seen that family remains an important source of values as young people mature, and so do friends for non-churchgoers. For churchgoing Gen Xers church continues to be a strong source of values, in fact the highest, but it drops out of significance for non-churchgoers. Non-churchgoers in both age groups rate the media as a much stronger source of values than do churchgoers, but teachers seem to be rated worse in retrospect than they are during school life.

When using this method of evaluation the discussion is usually fascinating as respondents try to come to some agreement. There were three areas of debate in these groups, but interestingly very little discussion about church as a source of values – it just *is* the source for spiritual values!

- Should family and friends be placed as equally important? Family were recognised as giving you the values "you grow up with". But friends were important as the people with whom you decided which of those family values you wished to retain and which to change. After some fairly heated discussion, both groups finally agreed to put family first and friends close behind.

- How important are teachers as a source of values? They were seen much more as a source of knowledge than of values by the churchgoing group, hence the lower score. There was a definite difference between younger Tweenagers and older in this, with the younger ones wanting a higher score for teachers than the older ones.
- How much influence do the media actually have? Initial suggestions ranged from 1 (virtually no influence) to 9 (very strong influence), with the general opinion eventually being that the media might influence some people but it didn't affect them very much, because they judged the media by the values they learned from elsewhere. Hopefully that is true, but the facilitator (who has an MTh in the Theology and Ethics of Communication) is rather sceptical as this contradicts media research from other sources.

Reasons for such behaviour

It may be asked why Tweenagers should indulge in such behaviour. An article by Dr John Coleman, Director of the Trust for the Study of Adolescence, suggested that because young people cannot be economically independent until their early twenties because of studying, they "turn to other means to exhibit adult behaviour, such as drinking, drug-taking and sex"[22].

Younger Tweenagers see what older teenagers are doing, and copy it. Another article said "adolescence is characterised by 'risk taking behaviour'"[23], and part of that risk can be seen in drinking, smoking and drug-taking. Sadly, parental example may also be a factor, while peer pressure is perhaps the most deadly influence of all.

Part of the pressure, as we have already seen, is to experiment with sex. "A Government report, *Listen Up,* said girls' reputations were strongly influenced by their attitudes towards sex."[24] But that same pressure can also encourage drug-taking as well. Melvin Burgess wrote a book about a teenager who gave up her GCSEs to "have a sexual adventure fuelled by drink and drugs" because, he said, teenagers "appreciate real life, not a fairy tale."[25]

"Young people are at increasing risk of depression and other mental health disorders"[26] and "one child in five is now suspected to have mental health problems"[27]. More young women than young men, but still around two-fifths of all Tweenagers, agreed with the statement "I certainly feel useless at times" as shown in Figure 7.8[28]:

Figure 7.8: Tweenagers agreeing "I certainly feel useless at times" by age and gender

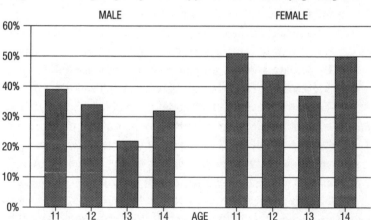

Low self-esteem is only one element of the pressure many Tweenagers feel under. And that pressure can lead to other behaviours to raise their self-esteem either in their own eyes or those of their friends – or their parents, as a survey undertaken by Altrincham Baptist Church found[29]. One article began, "Parents! Please Listen! Maybe it seems like I don't want your opinion. But I really do care about what you think."[30]

Drugs and drink don't only relate to self-esteem, however. Why get high? Some children replied, "To forget problems and become happy"[31], and while that came from a Third World street child, UK Tweenagers in some circumstances might well answer likewise.

Hurting someone

Earlier it was seen that 17% of the Tweenage respondents to this survey had intentionally tried to hurt someone physically in the previous three months. Some of this will be blatant bullying; how can such aggressive attitudes be healed? One article[32] suggests:
- Apologise privately to your former victims if possible
- Try to make amends or at least be pleasant to former victims
- See if you can help new people who may feel isolated
- Pursue other interests or develop new ones
- Take up a sport if you have lots of energy and can't sit still
- Learn how to control your anger and aggression
- If you have a friend you can trust, ask them for help
- Set yourself goals ("I won't bother John this morning")
- Talk to someone at school about the problem and see if there is a quiet place to go if feelings are getting the better of you
- Don't get disheartened. You won't become perfect overnight!

Sometimes the victims are siblings or stepbrothers or sisters living in the same home, or their boy or girlfriends. One NSPCC study of nearly 3,000 adults aged 18 to 24 asked about their childhood experiences. Nearly 10% had been attacked at home, violently. Three-quarters were attacked for the first time between the ages of 13 and 15. Such attacks were largely sexual, rape or oral sex, and came more from those approximately their own age rather than their parents or step-parents (43% stepbrother to 19% stepfather and 14% father)[33]. An American study showed that between 70% and 80% of sex offenders are known to the children, with such offences lasting on average three years[34]. Another headline was "Threat comes from family, not strangers in the street."[35]

There is another side, however. "Some 14 year olds want to have sex, not because they lack love or self-esteem, but because they're human and they feel like it."[36] Nor must it be assumed that all such improper behaviour, sexual or otherwise, is outside the church. Unfortunately not[37]. There are many stories in the papers of clerical misconduct, but lay misconduct is equally or more prevalent though usually not so publicised. The impact of such behaviour has been the subject of some research[38]. Where there are ways of minimising the risk of abuse in churches they should be taken.

So where does this all take us?

This chapter has shown that:
- A majority of Tweenagers felt stealing and cheating was always wrong. 71% disagreed that it was OK to take things like pencils from school, and 45% that it was OK to copy from other people. Honesty was an important issue for them.
- A majority also felt it was sometimes necessary to lie and that the main purpose in life was enjoyment and personal fulfilment.
- Two-fifths, 38%, of Tweenagers undertook an activity to help others near where they lived, a percentage which mostly decreased by age although 14 year olds were higher than 13 year olds.
- Almost three-fifths, 58%, of Tweenagers would keep a £20 note if found, but only two-fifths, 40%, would keep £100 if they found it.
- A quarter, 24%, would hand in £20 if they found it to a police station, but two-fifths, 42%, would hand in £100.
- These views varied greatly according to a Tweenager's age, gender, grades usually achieved, frequency s/he accessed the internet, and church attendance. Of these the factor achieving the greatest difference in practical behaviour was whether or not Tweenagers went regularly to church.
- More than half of all Tweenagers had watched a horror film or lied to an adult in the previous three months, while just under a half had lied to another young person.

- A smaller proportion, at most one-fifth, had undertaken a number of other illegal or undesirable actions in the previous three months. The incidence of several of these increased with age.
- Generally the proportions who said they had smoked, taken illegal drugs, or drunk too much were similar to Government figures where available.
- Some regular churchgoing Tweenagers had also undertaken similar activities, but less so than those who never attended church.
- Tweenagers recognise their family as a primary source of their values, but are in the process of shaping their own values mainly in relation to their friends. They are not in agreement about whether teachers have much influence on them, but take 'church' for granted as a source of spiritual values.
- Others have shown that part of the reason Tweenagers act in this way is the pressure put upon them, their need for self-esteem among their peers, and the fear of violence from those they know at home, often step-siblings more than adults.
- On the other hand, there are some who engage in these various activities, especially sex, because they feel adult and misguidedly wish to do so.

While honesty is a critical element of a Tweenager's value systems, other factors such as age and church attendance also make a huge difference. The regularity of churchgoing makes the greatest impact on values, a finding endorsed by others, but it is also greater than demographic variations.

The years from 10 to 14 are a period of great change, but the greatest changes take place usually about the ages of 11 and 12. Those aged 14 are often either about the same as those aged 13, or maybe a percentage point or two against the overall trend, suggesting a modest reappraisal of values then, or at least a desire not to change more. The first two years at secondary school are therefore critical in shaping values.

NOTES

[1] A true story told by the boy's grandfather, Brad Walden, Lexington, Kentucky, and related in *Leadership* magazine, Spring 2001, Page 71.

[2] *Cheating Yourself,* Teens talk about the choice between right and wrong, *Christopher News Notes,* New York, editor Stephanie Raha, Number 438, January 2002.

[3] His book *Churchgoing and Christian Ethics,* Cambridge University Press, 1999, contains many examples linking frequency of churchgoing with moral attitudes and behaviour.

[4] *Winning Them Back,* Eddie Gibbs, MARC, Tunbridge Wells, Kent, 1993.

[5] From *SoulSalsa,* Leon@rd Sweet, Zondervan, 2000, Page 33.

[6] Likewise those who had been baptised as infants were twice as likely to help others through the church than those who had not (27% to 13%).

[7] In the Ansvar Survey of English Social Behaviour, reported in *Religious Trends* No 1, 1998/1999, Paternoster Publishing, Carlisle, and Christian Research, London, edited by Peter Brierley, Pages 5.6 and 5.7.

[8] Ibid., so did the Ansvar results.

[9] Details in Chapter 4.

[10] *Social Focus on Young People,* National Statistics, The Stationery Office, Norwich, 2000, Table 2.16, Page 30.

[11] Article "Cigarettes and alcohol and young people" by Tim Stamp in *Horizons,* Issue 19, Autumn 2001, Page 10.

[12] Article "False smoke alarm" in the *Evening Standard,* 27 July 2001, Page 15.

[13] Article "Are you prepared for puberty?" by Sue Woodman in *Family Life,* June, July 2001, Page 60, as given on September 2001; website www.nvapress.com/ctt

[14] Ibid., Table 2.18, Page 31.

[15] Report "Drunk, doped up and still in school" by Thomas Harding in the *Daily Telegraph,* 21 February 2001, Page 4.

[16] Article "Children aged 13 are binge drinking" by Philip Johnston in the *Daily Telegraph,* 8 April 2002, Page 9.

[17] *Social Trends Quarterly,* Pilot Issue, Winter 1998, Page 5, and quoted in *Steps to the Future,* Scripture Union and Christian Research, London, 2000, Page 52.

[18] Report "Child use of drink, drugs and tobacco on increase" describing a Department of Health report, by Nicole Martin in the *Daily Telegraph,* 27 July 2001, Page 12.

[19] Taken from *Sociology Update 2001,* Professor Martyn Denscombe, Olympus Books UK, 2001, Page 17.

[20] *Drug Use, Smoking and Drinking among Teenagers in 1999,* was undertaken jointly by the Department of Health and the Home Office, and covered 9,000 young people aged 11 to 15 in 340 schools in England.

[21] *Knowledge and experience of drug use amongst church-affiliated young people,* by Christopher Cook, Deborah Goddard and Rachel Westall, Evangelical Alliance, London, 1997, and also quoted in *Idea,* June–August 1996, Page 1 and *Steps to the Future,* 2000, Page 52. 7,600 teenagers over 12 were interviewed.

[22] Article in the *Independent,* 29 May 2001, Page 14.

[23] Article "Teenagers and Sex" by Debbie Mountjoy, in *Zadok Perspectives,* No 45, July 1994, Page 4.

[24] Article "Girl Power fails to solve sex problems" by Marie Woolf in the *Daily Telegraph*, 12 April 2000.

[25] *Lady, My Life as a Bitch* by Melvin Burgess, published September 2001, and article "Children should read my tale of teen lust" in the *Daily Telegraph* by Kitty Melrose, 7 August 2001, Page 3.

[26] *The Burden of Youth*, The Henley Centre and the Salvation Army, 2001, Page 47.

[27] Op cit., (Footnote 22).

[28] Op cit., (Footnote 26).

[29] 1998 survey by Danny Brierley, when Youth Worker at the church.

[30] *Teen Dating*, What you need to know, Christopher News Notes, New York, Number 428, 2001.

[31] Article "Street children and substance misuse" by Premila Pavamani in *Reaching Children at Risk*, Viva Network, Oxford, Volume 5, Issue 1, February 2001, Page 9.

[32] Article "I sometimes bully people, what can I do?" reprinted from *Kidscape* in *Reaching Children at Risk*, Viva Network, Oxford, Volume 2, Issue 1, May 1998, Page 14.

[33] Article "One in 10 teenagers is victim of violent sex" by Nicole Martin in the *Daily Telegraph*, 1st March 2001, Page 9, reporting survey of 2,869 adults by NSPCC, details on www.nspcc.org.uk

[34] Box "The painful truth" in an article "Safe at church" by Beth Lueders in *Leadership*, Volume XVIII, Number 3, Summer 1997, Page 100.

[35] Article by Philip Johnston in the *Daily Telegraph*, 27 November 1997.

[36] Article "Underage sex and the modern facts of life" by Zoe Williams in the *Evening Standard*, 27 July 2001, Page 15.

[37] See article "Abuse in Ministry", by Patricia Fouque, *Ministry Today*, Richard Baxter Institute for Ministry, Essex, Issue 10, June 1997, Page 6.

[38] See, for example, the article "A national survey of the sexual trauma experiences of Catholic Nuns" in *Review of Religious Research*, Volume 40, Number 2, December 1998, Page 142, and also mentioned in *Religious Trends* No 2, 2000/2001, Christian Research and HarperCollins, London, 1999, Page 5.3.

CHAPTER EIGHT

What do Tweenagers believe?

Native Americans trained young braves in a special way. "On the night of a boy's 13th birthday, after learning hunting, scouting, and fishing skills, he was placed in a dense forest to spend the entire night alone. Until then he had never been away from the security of the family and tribe. But on this night he was blindfolded and taken several miles away. When he took off the blindfold, he was in the middle of thick woods. By himself. All night long.

"Every time a twig snapped, he visualised a wild animal ready to pounce. Every time an animal howled, he imagined a wolf leaping out of the darkness. Every time the wind blew, he wondered what more sinister sound it masked. It was a terrifying night.

"After what seemed like an eternity, dawn broke and the first rays of sunlight entered the interior of the forest. Looking around, the boy saw flowers, trees, and the outline of the path. Then to his utter astonishment, he beheld the figure of a man standing just a few feet away, armed with a bow and arrow.

"It was the boy's father. He had been there all night long. Can you think of any better way for a child to learn how God allows us to face the tests of life? God is always present with us. God's presence is unseen, but it is more real that life itself."[1]

In the film *The Matrix* Morpheus describes the Matrix, the imaginary world in which human beings are living, as "The world that has been pulled over your eyes to blind you from the truth."[2] The final part of the Tweenager survey looked at their beliefs and experiences: how much had a world been pulled over their eyes?

slightly more Tweenagers who believed in heaven than in G̲o̲d̲. ̲T̲his apparent irregularity (from a Christian viewpoint) has been sometimes observed before and is not confined to young people[3]:

Attitude	This survey %	Gallup Poll: 1990s average %
Heaven	73	52
God	72	67
Jesus	67	49
Hell	50	25
The Devil	43	26
Reincarnation	28	25

From the Gallup polls averages for adults it may be concluded that Tweenagers have higher levels of spiritual belief than those the age of their parents[4]. How far this is due to the greater spirituality expressed by many at the turn of the 21st century than in the decade before, or to their younger age (not yet disillusioned?), or to the characteristics of this particular sample (which included a much higher percentage of regular churchgoers than in the general population) is not known, but is probably due in part to each.

Tweenager answers varied by their Christian commitment, as might be expected. Details are given in Table A4/33, but show:

- Those who are sure they are Christian have a higher percentage of traditional beliefs than those who are not sure where they stand. The latter have a stronger belief in reincarnation.
- Those who are no longer Christian tend to believe at the lower levels of those who have never been Christian, except for reincarnation in which 47% of ex-Christians believe (against 35% of those who have never been Christian).

- While ex-Christians and those who have never been Christian are much less likely to believe in heaven, God or Jesus, they are only slightly less likely to believe in hell and the devil.
- Those of other religions are very likely to believe in God, but much less likely to believe in Jesus or the Devil.

Tweenager belief did not vary by gender except that young women believed in heaven more than men (58% to 42%). Belief in heaven, God and Jesus did however vary by age, as illustrated in Figure 8.1. The graph shows that belief declines between ages 10 and 13 (through their transition to secondary school), but (for God and heaven) increases again slightly when 14.

Figure 8.1: Tweenager belief by age

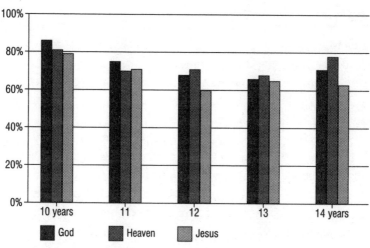

Likewise, Tweenager belief was higher for those who generally obtained higher grades at school[5]. The broad levels of belief are lower than they were in the early 1990s for older teenagers, but not greatly different. For example, belief in God and Jesus then was 82% and 74% respectively (against 72% and 67% here) for those aged 16 to 19 in a survey published in 1992[6].

Tweenager belief naturally varied with the frequency of church attendance, with regular attenders having much higher levels of belief[7]. The main factor in belief is between those who attend regularly and those who go less often[8]. Average belief in heaven, God and Jesus was 93% for regular churchgoers against 72% for occasional churchgoers, and although this again reinforces Robin Gill's thesis, it also shows that the largest differences in belief are between the committed and the less committed (as indicated by church attendance), as other differences are all much smaller.

The same kind of difference emerged between those who felt secure and loved at home (whether always or only sometimes) where belief in God and Jesus averaged 74% and 68% respectively against 57% and 52% for those who were uncomfortable at home or didn't live in a close, loving family.

In other words, high levels of spiritual belief tend to be associated with regular churchgoing, Christian commitment, home security, academic capability and to some extent with age. Confidence in spiritual things is associated with confidence in other aspects of a Tweenager's life. This explains why their spiritual poise can be so affected if, say, their parents' divorce.

Thus in a world which is increasingly insecure, spiritual belief is harder to sustain. An alternative thesis would suggest that beyond a certain point, disillusionment with the violent, lawless state of the world leads to spiritual hunger and search for belief, if not the truth.

Is one reason for the decline in churchgoing the deterioration seen in societal behaviour over the 1990s? On the other hand, it might be argued that deterioration in societal behaviour is a result rather than the *cause* of the decline in churchgoing.

Teenage belief (in God at least) is changing. In 1994 the 16% of 12–19 year olds who "didn't believe in God and never have" rose to 26% by 1998, and the 45% who "believe in God now and always have" dropped to 37%[9]. Are these the marks of a post-Christian society?

It is easy to look at percentages who believe in God or heaven and feel that this constitutes the big picture. In reality it doesn't.

Such percentages relate only to a specific time and circumstance, and vary not only over the years, but over the increasing age of a child, between genders and social class, between those attending church schools and those not doing so (a variation not considered in this study), between differing homes and parental attitudes, and on the personalities of those involved (an attribute also not considered here). They vary by denomination and churchmanship, by societal culture and religious experience. Few have attempted to complete the whole jigsaw[10], and what is presented in the rest of this chapter is but parts of a much wider picture, summarised at the end, and from which tentative conclusions are drawn.

One pair of researchers has described children as living "in not two but three worlds: that of their extraction which provides traditional values and beliefs in which they are instructed, the modernist world of rationally-orientated progress and socio-economic ambition, and the more individual world of personal well-being and freedom. In part these worlds might well overlap, but their balance can easily be disturbed in favour of one of the first two. The axis which enables the child to orientate themselves successfully, however, is in fact the third."[11] "Well-being" has been found to vary by type of school[12].

Been baptised or confirmed?

Over half, 55%, said they had been christened and 40% said they had been baptised, perhaps more as infants than in "believer's baptism" but the question didn't specify. They are both much higher than the national percentage of children who are baptised within the first year of life, 35% in 1999[13], because a significant proportion of the sample came from churched young people who (if Anglican, Catholic or Methodist) would be likely to have been christened or baptised. While the large majority of Church of England baptisms are for babies, there were 2,300 for young people aged 10 to 13 in 1994, and 1,100 for those aged 14 to 17, only 2% of the total[14]. Catholics were more likely than Evangelicals to have been baptised between 10 and 13, but Evangelicals more likely than Catholics for those aged 14 to 17[15].

A fifth, 19%, had been admitted to (or had gone to) communion. These were much more likely to say that knowing Jesus as their personal Saviour made someone a Christian and to have been admitted as a member of their church. Those who had taken communion were much more likely to be regular churchgoers (72% to 28%), and less likely to have watched a horror or violent film in the previous three months (41% to 28% who had not taken communion).

One sixth, 16%, had been confirmed, and a further sixth, 15%, had been admitted to membership of a church. Both, as might be expected, increased with age. The jump for both was also quite marked: 17% of those aged 13 had been confirmed, but 30% of those aged 14; 11% of those aged 13 had been admitted into church membership, but 21% of those aged 14.

In 1994 the total number of young people aged 10 to 13 confirmed in the Church of England was 17,600, and aged 14 to 17 8,600, together being 56% of the total that year[16]. Confirmees and church members were twice as likely to attend church regularly than non-confirmees or non-members (61% to 32% and 66% to 31% respectively). Confirmees are more likely per capita of the population in rural areas, and also more likely to be male, under 14[17], and to be associated with a growing church.

Baptism (as an infant or a believer) was seen as an indication of being a Christian by those *who had not been baptised.* Seven-eighths, 88%, of the 257 respondents who said they had never been a Christian had not been baptised, whereas 53% who said they were Christians had been. Likewise those who had been baptised were more likely to attend church regularly (49% against 28% who had not been); those not baptised were nearly three times more likely not to have been to church at all (31% to 12%). So baptism counts for something, and indicates the importance that many churches place in keeping rolls and registers and following up those who come for infant baptism, or welcoming believers into full membership.

Think about God?

Almost three-fifths, 58%, of Tweenagers said they thought about whether or not God existed, and almost half, 45%, believed a relationship with Him was possible. A quarter, 24% and 25% respectively, answered NO to both questions, leaving a sixth, 18%, unsure about whether God existed and a third, 30%, unsure about a relationship. There was a significant correlation[18] between these two answers – those who thought God existed tended to believe in a relationship.

Christian Tweenagers were more likely to think about God than those who were not. Likewise, three-quarters, 74%, of the few Hindus in the sample and two-thirds of the Sikhs and Jews, 67% and 60% respectively, also thought about whether God exists, but only a half, 46%, of the small number of Muslims[19].

Pictures of God

What picture of God did Tweenagers have? They were as follows, with the figures in square brackets being the average results of those aged 11 to 14 in the *Reaching and Keeping Teenagers* survey of 1992:

• 62% Creator	[68%]
• 61% Father	[56%]
• 56% Friend	[—]
• 48% Love	[60%]
• 35% Saviour	[41%]
• 35% Old Man	[31%]
• 22% Judge	[27%]
• 9% Mother	[10%]
• 5% Policeman	[3%]
• 4% Spoilsport	[4%]
• 9% Other	[7%]

This list shows virtually the same order of importance as in 1992 (only the position of Love varies) and on the whole very similar percentages, the largest difference being the picture of God as

Love. In 1992 Love and Father were very close; in 2001 Father has become more important than Love. Could this reflect the changing roles of father (and stepfathers) in the interim, or could it reflect the different levels of importance of father for Tweenagers and teenagers? In the 1992 study Love was ticked by 62% females and 47% males; in 2001 these percentages were 56% and 44% respectively, showing that the perception of God as Love has decreased more among the females.

The 1992 study did not include the word "Friend", which emerges as the third most important picture in 2001. Tweenagers could tick as many choices as they wished; on average they ticked seven for every two people. Three have slightly larger percentages since 1992 – Father, Old Man and Policeman. Table A4/36 gives figures by school year for Father, and they show a decline as the Tweenager gets older, though with an upturn at age 14. (The same is true for Friend, the only other picture to vary with age).

Table 8.2 shows the variations in the picture of God by church-going frequency and degree of religious commitment. The pictures of Mother and Policeman did not vary by either, so are omitted.

Table 8.2: Picture of God by church attendance and Christian commitment

	Church attendance				Religious Commitment					
Picture	Regular %	Occasional %	Lapsed %	Never %	Certain %	Unsure %	Lapsed %	Never %	Another religion %	Overall %
Creator	84	65	60	42	78	61	31	34	59	62
Father	83	59	55	34	76	54	25	32	33	61
Friend	79	52	47	30	69	49	8	28	41	56
Love	73	47	41	27	64	42	10	22	42	48
Saviour	60	30	27	18	50	28	8	15	18	35
Old Man	24	39	48	48	32	43	50	53	19	35
Judge	32	22	24	12	29	21	15	11	26	22
Spoilsport	2	3	6	9	3	6	6	10	1	4

The highlighted boxes are where the percentage is 20% or more different (either way) from the overall percentage. It may thus be immediately seen that:

- Regular churchgoing is important for positive pictures of God
- Those who have never been to church lack a whole category of perceptions of who God is
- Those who are no longer Christian (who invariably have the lowest percentages) have largely rejected, and those who have never been Christian have never had positive images of God (as given by the first five words)
- Those who belong to another religion do not have a similar understanding of the fatherhood of God as Christians do.

Some of the pictures varied by the school grade usually obtained, or the type of home in which a Tweenager lived, given in Table A4/37, but none varied as much as in Table 8.2. Leslie Francis has shown that the images of God held by 13 to 15 year olds are important for shaping their personal and social worldview[20].

Who was Jesus Christ?

Two-thirds, 68%, of respondents said Jesus Christ was the Son of God, which is higher than the 49% given by adults in Gallup surveys[21], as found already with other belief questions. It is also higher than the 47% found by Leslie Francis in a large teenage survey[22]. One in every eight, 13%, thought He was a very wise person, 11% someone who never existed, and 8% an ordinary person.

As might be expected, a much higher percentage of Christian Tweenagers, 84%, believed that Jesus was the Son of God, but even so this only represents five Christian Tweenagers in every six. Those who had given up their Christianity had no common mind on who Jesus was, except that He was not the Son of God (19%, other options equally split). A third, 32%, of those who were not Christian said Jesus never existed.

As with other belief questions, the proportion believing Jesus was the Son of God decreased with age, from 80% of those aged 10 down to 60% of those aged 13, but rising to 68% for those 14 years old, as can be seen in Figure 8.3:

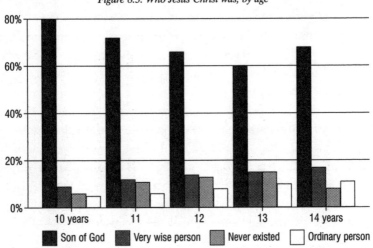

Figure 8.3: Who Jesus Christ was, by age

Doubts of Jesus' existence seem to diminish as Tweenagers get older, being replaced by Him being considered as an ordinary man or a wise person. Girls were more likely to consider Jesus as the Son of God (73% to 63%) and boys that He never existed (14% to 9%).

Nine-tenths, 91%, of regular churchgoers accepted Jesus as the Son of God, but then so did two-fifths, 42%, of those who had never been to church. Consideration of who Jesus was at the time of the survey varied by the age at which those who had been attending Sunday School or Junior Church stopped doing so, as shown in Figure 8.4.

The longer a child spent in Sunday School the more likely they were to believe that Jesus was the Son of God, but doubts as to His "ordinariness" seem to persist, and a few were never sure He existed.

Those who had been baptised were more likely to think that Jesus was the Son of God (77% to 63% not baptised), whereas those not baptised were twice as likely to think Jesus never existed (14% to 6%). The same was true for those who had been admitted to communion – 85% said Jesus was the Son of God compared to 65% not yet admitted, and for those who had been confirmed – 82% to 66%.

Figure 8.4: Who Jesus Christ was, by age of leaving Sunday School

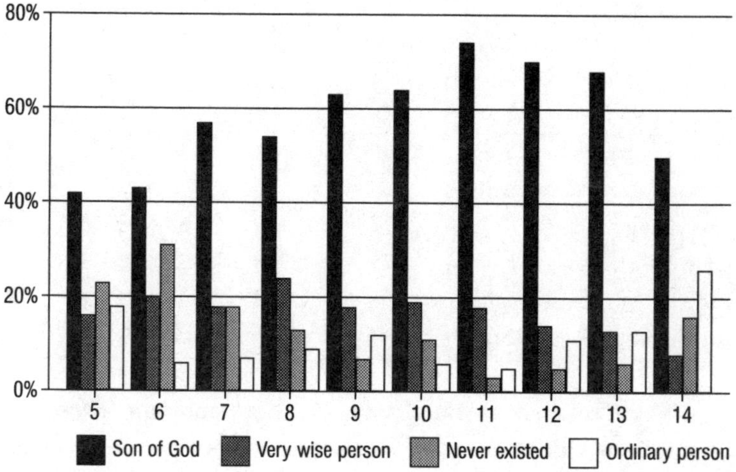

Where do we go when we die?

The most common reaction was consistent with perceived Christian teaching, but not the remainder:

- 35% Good people go to heaven and bad people go to hell
- 19% Everyone goes to heaven
- 15% Nothing, everything just stops
- 13% Only Christians go to heaven
- 10% People die and are born again as someone else
- 8% People die and are born again as another creature

The total for the last two items, 18%, is rather less than the 28% who indicated they believed in reincarnation. Perhaps they believed in reincarnation as well as God![23] Those believing that everyone goes to heaven became fewer the older they were, and, conversely, those thinking everything just stops increased with age[24]. These two statements elicited significant gender differences, for reasons not clear, with girls tending to believe everyone went to heaven (22% to 16% men) and boys that everything stops (20% to 11%).

A Tweenager's Church attendance naturally made a difference to his/her answers, as Table 8.5 indicates:

Table 8.5: Belief by church attendance

I believe...	Regular %	Occasional %	Lapsed %	Never %	Overall %
Good people go to heaven...	39	34	14	24	35
Everyone goes to heaven	23	16	8	11	19
Everything just stops	7	19	38	36	15
Only Christians go to heaven	19	8	2	2	13
People reborn as someone else	8	14	14	14	10
People reborn as a creature	4	9	24	14	8

The frequency of churchgoing is again important. Those who have left the church are more likely to believe everything just stops (as do those who have never been) or that people are reincarnated as another creature.

Those who lose their parents while they are still children can find their belief systems uncertain. An excellent article urges schools "to take on board bereavement issues, both in individual counselling and in group therapy."[25] An orphanage for 50 children in Kisumu, Kenya encourages the children to talk about their loss to each other and to visitors very openly; this helps them come to terms with who and where they are.

Becoming a Christian

What makes a person a Christian? Ten specific answers were suggested, with opportunity to add others. The most common answer was given by two-thirds, 70%, of Tweenagers as "Believing in God".

Girls were more likely than boys (75% to 65%) to think that believing in God made someone a Christian.

Tweenagers could tick as many as they wished. There were seven ticks for every two respondents. The full list of answers was:

- 70% Believing in God
- 53% Being baptised/christened
- 52% Believing the Bible is true
- 45% Knowing Jesus as a personal saviour[26]
- 36% Going to church
- 29% Being born in a Christian family
- 26% Leading a good life
- 21% Saying that they are Christian
- 15% Going to a Christian school
- 3% Being born in the UK
- 3% Something else
- 7% Don't know

Some of these varied by the frequency with which Tweenagers went to church. Table A4/38 gives details, and shows that those going to church regularly were more likely to think that believing in God, believing the Bible to be true, and knowing Jesus as personal Saviour made one a Christian. They were less likely to think that being baptised, being born in a Christian family or going to a Christian school did the trick. Answers from those who only attended occasionally, who had stopped going or who had never gone were always very similar to each other. A minority thought people could become Christian in other ways[27].

Knowing Christ as Saviour is important, but what are the chances of that happening? George Barna in the United States has estimated[28] that of those aged 5 to 13, a third, 32%, are probably likely to find Him. Of those aged 14 to 18, he reckons only 4% are likely to do so, and of aged 19 or older, a fifth, 19%. How far these figures apply to the UK is not known, but the sharp decrease between 5 to 13 and 14 to 18 is **very** likely to be true here also. The imperative therefore is to reach young people *young* and to be more effective in the mid-years!

Some have criticised these percentages, but a study of 369 Christian students on ten American college campuses confirmed them. It also indicated that the process of conversion took place over a long period and that "there was a critical recommitment of their lives to Christ, which they regarded as significant as their conversion itself... Their biggest time of doubt came during their teenage years."[29] While this emphasises that conversion is not simply an event, it also indicates the importance of laying a foundation on which later spiritual happenings can build[30].

Religious experience

The opportunity was taken to ask Tweenagers about other kinds of religious experience they may have had, and their answers are given in Table 8.6.

Table 8.6: Occurrence of different types of religious experience

Experienced any of these?	YES %	Not sure %	NO %
Visions/voices/strange dreams	38	17	45
A feeling of peace during a church service	38	20	42
An experience of becoming a Christian	35	29	36
The presence of God	32	26	42
Somebody/something trying to communicate	31	24	45
Something beyond description	23	22	55
An experience to do with nature	22	28	50
Some other spiritual/supernatural force	20	26	54
A healing experience	15	25	60
Something else	7	11	82
Average	26	23	51

The average percentage doesn't mean much except to say that about half of these Tweenagers do not claim to have any of these spiritual experiences, and about a quarter of them have. The remaining quarter are uncertain. In 1992 the percentages for teenagers were, respectively, 26%, 39% and 35%[31], showing that a more recent and younger generation are less likely (or less likely yet[32]) to have had any religious experience.

Those who said they experienced visions or voices or strange dreams declined with age, from 48% having them when aged 10 to 30% when aged 14. Five-eighths, 63%, of those who said they had experienced peace during a church service had been admitted to communion. A feeling of peace during a church service, an experience of becoming a Christian and the presence of God were all much more likely to be experienced by those attending church regularly and much much less likely to have been experienced by those who never went (highlighted boxes in Table A4/39); in other words these are experiences likely to be only had, or seen to be had, in the context of a church.

The fifth, 22%, who said they had had a religious experience to do with nature compares with 15% of Gen Xers in a 2001 survey[33]. Could this suggest that younger people are more likely to have such religious experiences? A quarter, 27%, of those with this experience had been baptised compared with 19% who had not had a natural experience. Might baptism be seen as making a Tweenager more spiritually aware? Or conversely, had Teenagers with some kind of religious experience then sought baptism? The highest percentage feeling they had had an experience with nature, 27%, were those who only went to church occasionally (Table A4/39).

The respect for nature is important: The Australian Wiccan, Fiona Horne, wrote *Life's a Witch!*, especially aimed for teenagers[34]. In it she writes, "I dig Jesus!... if he was around today, with his values of tolerance, acceptance, respect for Nature [capital sic] and fellow people, he'd be a Witch!"[35] Note the concern is for what Jesus did, not who He was.

Did the respondents know anybody who had had experiences like these? Half, 47%, said they did. How had they reacted to them or their experience? Three in every seven, 42%, said they could relate to it, but one in seven, 15%, said they thought it was scary, and a like proportion, 14%, thought such people were a bit mad[36]! Of the other two-sevenths, half were either envious (7%) or thought it was a coincidence (5%), and the rest had other reactions.

These ranged from believing such experiences were true, to being uncertain or simply not understanding, but feeling they were normal and the experience for such people was valid. Those who were Christians were much more likely to be able to relate to others having such religious experiences; those in other religions were more likely to find them scary.

Is Christianity relevant?

The final question asked, "Do you think Christianity is relevant for you?" Half of the respondents, 52%, said YES, with a quarter, 21%, negative, and the remaining quarter, 27%, unsure. Girls were more likely to feel it was relevant for them than boys, 55% to 49%.

Naturally most of those who went to church regularly thought Christianity was relevant to them, but only 85%, suggesting, as with previous questions, that there is a small minority in church who do not feel that it is relevant for them. These, one presumes, are those most likely to leave. Likewise, only 78% of those who said they knew they were Christian felt Christianity was relevant for them!

Does this indicate an anomaly between belief and experience, that is, giving mental assent to Christian truths but failing to find them making any difference to daily living? Could it be a communication issue in that what is being taught is not necessarily what is understood? 17% of these said they weren't sure if Christianity was relevant, and 5% said it definitely wasn't – is that because it used to be but was less so now, or because they are not sure right now, but it may be so in the future? These percentages and those for respondents not sure of their Christianity are illustrated in Figure 8.7:

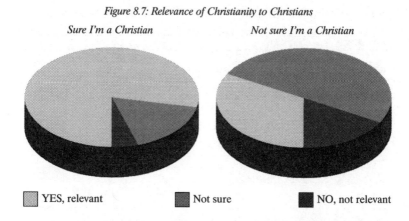

Figure 8.7: Relevance of Christianity to Christians

Sure I'm a Christian   *Not sure I'm a Christian*

YES, relevant   Not sure   NO, not relevant

Figure 8.7 shows that relevance and Christian religious belief do not necessarily go together. This is not unique to Tweenagers, nor to the UK. In an Australian study "students" spoke of the irrelevance of organised religion to their lives... [but] claimed that spirituality was an important part."[37] A British study suggested that "a sense of spirituality is almost universal among children, but subsequent feelings of embarrassment over such matters may be the main reason why people appear to lose faith as they grow older."[38] "Young people are developing a strong sense of spirituality but this is taking place outside formal churches."[39]

This leads on the question of what constitutes "spirituality". An attempt to define spiritual development (not quite the same thing) in schools by 214 heads of Welsh primary schools was interesting[40]. Their answers are depicted in Figure 8.8 and show that they considered that the development of personal and community values, and the ability to form relationships with others (this last the management guru Charles Handy has called one part of "interpersonal intelligence"[41]) as key – in other words the primary "spiritual" focus was among their peers and society rather than wider questions of life, death and God. It would be interesting to know how far young people themselves agreed with these answers: a study among university students would suggest much the same factors and order of priority[42].

Figure 8.8: Definitions of spiritual development

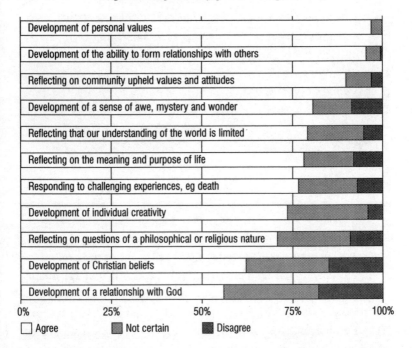

That over a fifth of Christian Tweenagers are already acknowledging that Christianity is not relevant to them (going back to Figure 8.7), or that they are uncertain, cannot be good news. Just as adults want relevance in their churches, so young people want relevance in their Sunday Schools and Youth Groups.

This is an American issue also. "Teens are not sure Christianity is the only way," ran a 2001 headline[43], quoting Christian apologist Josh McDowell as saying, "Christ is OK for now – until an experience tells teens that something better has come along." Hence the need to be in touch with Tweenager religious experiences, as already described.

Australians also have examined this issue and a useful summary of their findings has been published, describing the results of many researchers, but without coming to any overall conclusion[44].

Two-thirds, 64%, of those who normally obtained grade As felt Christianity was relevant to them, with 21% unsure, and 15% negative. For those getting grade Bs the percentages were, respectively, 46%, 30% and 24%, and for those getting grade Cs or lower they were 40%, 29% and 31%, showing a similar pattern seen elsewhere that those with higher grades feel more attracted to Christianity than those with lower grades. Is this simply a reflection of their social class?

Two-thirds, 66%, of those who had been baptised felt Christianity was relevant to them, and four-fifths, 80%, of those who had been admitted to communion. The latter high figure would support (Anglican) advocates of allowing young people to take communion, even if they have not yet been confirmed (Catholic children make their first Communion when 7 or 8 and are confirmed perhaps seven years later). Only 74% of confirmees felt Christianity was relevant!

What does "relevant" mean in this context? In some ways, the crux revolves around the person of Jesus Christ. Those for whom Christianity is relevant affirm that Jesus Christ is the Son of God (69%), whereas only 8% do so of those who feel Christianity is not relevant for them. The latter are much more likely to believe that Jesus was someone who does not exist (73%) or was an ordinary person (49%). This suggests our Sunday Schools should be helping young people to understand that Jesus really lived, was an extraordinary person and is the Son of God.

Knowing that Jesus is the Son of God is of course crucial. But is that all young people need to know? In his brilliant book on modern values, simply called *Blue,* Nick Page says that in his interview with Jesus Pilate got his three questions right[45]: "Are you the King?", "What have you done?", "What is the truth?" – in effect seeking to know His authority, actions and authenticity. This is what today's Tweenagers need to know as well.

So where does all this take us?

This chapter has shown:
- Three-quarters of Tweenagers believe in heaven and in God, and two-thirds in Jesus. However, what they believe about Jesus is critical for their perception of the relevance of Christianity to them.
- As elsewhere, gender is significant. Girls believe more than boys. There tends to be a decline in belief as Tweenagers get older, but a resurgence by the age of 14, suggesting that about age 13 may be the nadir of belief.
- Churchgoers naturally believe more than non-churchgoers. The frequency of attendance is also important, and confirms other research that belief follows frequency rather than vice versa. This reinforces the youth work dictum of "belong, believe, then behave".
- High levels of spiritual belief are associated with regular churchgoing, Christian commitment, home security and academic ability. Confidence in spiritual things is associated with confidence in other aspects of a Tweenager's life.
- Half the Tweenagers in this sample had been christened, higher than the national average because of the numbers of churchgoers in the survey. Baptism (as an infant christening or as a believer) was seen as an indication of being a Christian by those who had not been baptised, though not by those who had been baptised.
- Almost three-fifths of Tweenagers thought about whether God existed, and almost half believed a relationship with Him was possible. It should be noted that these Tweenagers are not rejecting God, but are rather open to the possibility of His existence and His relevance to them.
- The most common pictures of God was as a creator, father and friend, displacing the picture of God as love which was in second place in 1992. While churchgoers held these positive images, non-churchgoers did not (which is not to say they had negative images). Those in other religions did not see God as father as strongly as Christians.

- Two-thirds of Tweenagers believed Jesus was the Son of God, but the view of Him as a wise or just ordinary person, or even someone who never existed, was quite strongly held as well, especially by those aged 13.
- A third of Tweenagers believed good people went to heaven when they died. For those who no longer went to church, or had never gone, annihilism was more strongly believed.
- Knowing Jesus as your personal Saviour came fourth in a list of how people became Christian. Top were believing in God, being baptised or christened and believing the Bible to be true.
- About a quarter of Tweenagers said they had had some kind of religious experience, of which the top four were visions, voices and strange dreams, a feeling of peace during a church service, an experience of becoming a Christian and the presence of God. The last three were only to be had, or seen to be had, in the context of a church.
- Half the Tweenagers said they knew someone who had had such experiences. Those who were Christians were much more likely to be able to relate to others having such religious experiences; those in other religions were more likely to find them scary.
- While half the respondents thought Christianity was relevant to them, roughly four-fifths did so who were regular churchgoers or who were Christians. This leaves a relatively high percentage of churchgoers and Tweenage Christians who are unsure if Christianity is relevant to them, along with many others whose present practices or beliefs are less formal.
- The crux would seem to revolve around the person of Jesus Christ: those for whom Christianity is relevant strongly affirm that Jesus Christ is the Son of God, whereas only a few do so who feel Christianity is not relevant for them. These are more likely to believe that Jesus was someone who does not exist or was an ordinary person.

NOTES

[1] Taken from *SoulSalsa*, Leon@rd Sweet, Zondervan, 2000, Page 23.

[2] Taken from *Living on Purpose*, Tom and Christine Sine, Monarch Books, Mill Hill, London, 2002, Page 31.

[3] In 1973 adults answering a Gallup survey gave answers which likewise seem illogical from a Christian viewpoint. Details in *The Becoming Church*, John Adair, SPCK, 1977, Page 43.

[4] A phenomenon also noted by Professor Leslie Francis in his research.

[5] Table A4/34 shows the variation.

[6] Chapter 22 "What is a Christian? Investigating the understanding of 16 to 19 year olds" by Leslie Francis, Carolyn Wilcox and Jeff Astley in *The Contours of Christian Education*, edited by Jeff Astley and David Day, McCrimmon Publishing, Great Wakering, Essex, 1992.

[7] See Table A4/35 for details.

[8] Seen elsewhere also; cp *The Values Debate: A voice from the pupils* by Leslie Francis, Woburn Press, London, 2001, in which "only 41% of occasional churchgoers believe in God but 73% would like a church wedding" (taken from a review by Rev Peter Jackson in the *Church Times*, January 2002).

[9] Young People's Social Attitude Surveys, 1994 and 1998, National Centre for Social Research, quoted in *The Burden of Youth*, The Henley Centre and Salvation Army, London, 2001, Page 63.

[10] One such is Professor Leslie Francis. His paper "Attitudes towards Christianity during Childhood and Adolescence: Assembling the Jigsaw" in *The Journal of Beliefs and Values*, Volume 14, Number 2, 1993, Page 4, gives one particular overview which he has followed consistently.

[11] *Children's Constructions of Reality: Conceptual Expressions of Implicit Religion*, paper given by Clive Erricker and Cathy Ota of the Children and Worldviews Project, at the Network for the Study of Implicit Religion, Denton, May 1995, Page 21.

[12] Article "Helps to Fostering Students' Spiritual health" by John W Fisher, *International Journal of Children's Spirituality*, Volume 4, Number 1, June 1999, Page 34.

[13] *Religious Trends* No 3, Christian Research, London, 2001, Table 2.2.

[14] Figures taken from *Youth A Part*, Young people and the Church, National Society and Church House publishing, London, 1996, Page 94.

[15] Table 2 in two complementary publications, *In the Evangelical Way* and *In the Catholic Way*, by Leslie Francis and David Lankshear, The Church Union and the National Society, London, 1995, on Page 11 of both booklets.

[16] Ibid.

[17] Article "The Rural Church is different: the case of Anglican Confirmation" by Leslie Francis and David Lankshear, *Journal of Empirical Theology*, Volume 10, Number 1, 1997, Page 5. See also Table A4/40 in Appendix 4.

[18] $R = 0.17$, $P < 0.001$.

[19] Percentages based on those who answered the question amongst 20 Hindus, 10 Sikhs, 15 Jews, and 18 Muslims.

[20] Chapter "God images, personal well-being and moral values" by Leslie Francis in the book *Imagining God: Empirical explorations from an international perspective*, edited by Hans-George Ziebertz, Lit Verlag, Munster and London, 2001, Page 139.

[21] *Religious Trends* No 2, 2000/2001, Christian Research and HarperCollins, London, Table 5.9.1.

[22] *Teenage Religion and Values,* Leslie Francis and William Kay, Gracewing, Fowler Wright Books, Leominster, Herefordshire, 1995.

[23] Belief in reincarnation varies by background; those from ethnic backgrounds from the Indian sub-continent (for example, Indian Punjabis) were more likely to believe in reincarnation than those from white backgrounds, a finding consistent with other research, and in any case as might be expected. See also "Children and the World to Come: the Views of Children aged 8 to 14 in Life after Death" by Eleanor Nesbitt in *Religion Today,* Volume 8, Number 3, Summer 1993, Page 10.

[24] Belief in going to heaven decreased from 27% for those aged 10 to 19% for those aged 14, and everything just stopping increased from 9% to 15%.

[25] Article "Bereavement Group Therapy in School: the role of a belief in post-death existence within adolescent development for the acceptance process of loss" by Dennis Lines, *International Journal of Children's Spirituality,* Volume 4, Number 2, December 1999, Page 153.

[26] This is slightly higher than the 34% found for all teenagers in America, according to a report "Teenagers' beliefs moving farther from biblical perspectives", 23 October 2000 on www.barna.org

[27] Believing in Jesus (6 people), helping people (6), being confirmed (5), accepting God (5), knowing Jesus (5), loving God (5), praying to God (4), believing in God (4), repenting (4), asking for forgiveness (4), giving your life to God (4), believing in Christianity (3), believing in others (2), having faith (2), saying you are Christian (2), being afraid of the Devil (1), living by the Bible (1) and thinking we have a guardian angel (1 person).

[28] *Re-churching the unchurched,* George Barna, Issachar Resources, Ventura, California, 2000, Page 35.

[29] Article "The truth about evangelism" by Rick Lawrence, *Group,* Volume 26, Number 5, July/August 2000, Page 31, highlighted on www.navpress.com, October 2000.

[30] See, for example, *The Battle for a Generation,* Ron Hutchcraft, Moody Press, Chicago, 1996.

[31] *Reaching and Keeping Teenagers,* Peter Brierley, Monarch, Crowborough, 1992, Page 116.

[32] However, the 1992 study did not show any increase in religious experience with age, over the period 11 to 18 years of age.

[33] *Generation X: Attitudes and Lifestyle,* Christian and Non-Christian, undertaken for the Evangelical Alliance by Christian Research, London, 2001, by Peter Brierley.

[34] *Life's Witch! A Handbook for Teen Witches,* Fiona Horne, Random House Australia, Sydney, 2000.

[35] Ibid., taken from a review by Bill Stewart, Dean of Ridley College, University of Melbourne, in *Zadok Perspectives,* Number 73, Summer 2002, Page 24.

[36] Boys more than girls (20% to 10%), and those who were no longer or never had been Christian.

[37] *Religion in an Age of Change,* Peter H Ballis and Gary D Houma, Christian Research Association, Victoria, Australia, 1999, Page 85.

[38] Research reported in *Science and Spirit,* July/August 2000 but quotation taken from comment on it in *Religion Watch,* Volume 15, Number 10, September 2000, Page 4.

[39] Nick Bosanquet, quoted in *The Burden of Youth,* The Henley Centre and Salvation Army, London, 2001, Page 63.

[40] Article "What is Spiritual Development?" by G Davies in *International Journal of Children's Spirituality,* Volume 3, Number 2, December 1998, Page 129.

[41] *The Hungry Spirit,* Charles Handy, Hutchinson, London, Page 213.

[42] Op cit., (Footnote 37), Page 86.

[43] Article by Lee Weeks in *Pulpit Helps,* Volume 26, Number, January 2001, on July 2001 Current Thoughts & Trends Page of www.navpress.com

[44] *Youth Spirituality,* A summary of published research relating to youth spirituality, religiosity and values, Philip Hughes and Sharon Bond, prepared by the Christian Research Association, Uniting Education, Melbourne, Australia, 2001.

[45] *Blue,* Nick Page, HarperCollins, London, 2001, Page 66.

Tweenagers: where are they going?

The advertisement[1] was very clear: "It's impossible," says Reason. "It's reckless," says Experience. "It's painful," says Pride. "Try!" says Dream. The challenge... to bring a dream to life. This may be fine for Toyota, but Christians too need dreams... such as bringing Tweenagers to Christ. So let's try!

How do Tweenagers see themselves – and does it matter? Self-image is of major importance in forming a sense of well-being and self worth, so two questions were included on this vital topic.

Self-image

A list of 36 words was given and Tweenagers were invited to tick all they thought applied to themselves as individuals. On average they ticked one in every three, twelve per Tweenager. They saw themselves as being multi-faceted! Overall answers are given in Table 9.1:

Table 9.1: How Tweenagers saw themselves

Trait	%	Trait	%	Trait	%	Trait	%
Friendly	82	Sporty	52	Moody	28	Peaceful	15
Happy	67	Playful	49	Shy	27	Angry	14
Funny	64	Well-behaved	48	Unusual	26	Rude	14
Caring	63	Mature	45	Annoying	24	Scared	11
Helpful	57	Noisy	43	Ordinary	24	Perfect	10
Reliable	57	Messy	41	Leader	23	Slow	9
Talkative	57	Daring	36	Quiet	21	Self-centred	7
Hard-working	56	Lazy	36	Bossy	20	Unforgiving	7
Thoughtful	54	Forgetful	35	Fussy	20	Bully	3

Five Tweenagers in six, 82%, saw themselves as Friendly; this was their prime characteristic, which fits well with them being Mosaics or part of Generation Y. Two-thirds or thereabouts saw themselves as Happy, Funny and Caring, and somewhat over half thought they were Helpful, Reliable, Hard-working and Thoughtful, if Talkative! About half described themselves as Sporty, Playful and Well-behaved. Apart possibly from the word "talkative" these are all words with a positive sound or image, showing that the over-riding feeling these young people had of themselves was good.

Few of these varied with age, and none in the first column, except the last[2]. Those who saw themselves as Sporty or Playful declined as they got older, whereas the Mature, the Lazy and the Leader increased with age! The Unusual and Unforgiving peaked at age 12.

Self-image by gender

Rather more traits varied by gender, 14 out of the 36[3]. In 13 of these, the girls scored higher than the boys. The only trait in which the boys were higher than the girls was Sporty. In all the rest, the girls saw themselves in a more positive light. This concerned traits like being Friendly, Caring, Helpful, Reliable, Talkative, Hard-working, Thoughtful, Well-behaved and Mature. However, the girls also saw themselves as more Moody, Bossy, Fussy and Scared.

If this pattern is typical, which is very likely, it is no wonder that girls outperform boys. Their self image is markedly different. Does this explain why they are more confident in the early teenage years? It could also be due to hormonal changes and different routes of development through puberty.

There were two traits where the gender difference was especially noticeable: Caring and Talkative. Over three-quarters, 76%, of the girls described themselves as Caring, where only half, 50%, of the boys did so. Two-thirds, 68%, of the girls said they were Talkative, but just under half, 46%, of the boys. What does this "caring" trait mean in reality? Does it help explain their concern for friendship? Their pain when the home breaks up?

Self-image by ability

Even more traits varied with the grades normally obtained at school[4]. 17 out of the 36 listed varied in this way. Of these, ten decreased as grades went down. So young people who got As rather than Cs or lower were more likely to think they were Friendly, Caring, Helpful, Reliable, Hard-working, Thoughtful, Well-behaved, Mature, a Leader and Peaceful.

On the other hand, young people who got grades C or lower were more likely to feel they were Noisy, Lazy, Angry, Rude, Slow, Unforgiving or a Bully. These results at least give the suggestion that the answers were perceptively given, in other words, young people knew what they were like, and described themselves honestly.

Of the 36 characteristics listed, 11 show no variation by age, gender, or classroom ability. These are those who are Happy, Funny, Messy, Daring, Forgetful, Shy, Annoying, Ordinary, Quiet, Perfect or Self-centred. Only one varies by all three characteristics – those who are Mature. Do their traits vary other than by demographic factors like gender or ability? The answer was a little, but not as much, nor as significantly. Gender and ability were the key factors.

Self-image by spiritual factors

There were seven characteristics which varied by whether or not a Tweenager was Christian[5], four positive, three negative. The four positive (Caring, Helpful, Hard-working and Well-behaved) had the highest scores for those who were Christian or who belonged to another religion, lower scores for those not sure they were Christian or who had never been one, and the lowest scores for those who were no longer Christian. This suggests that in giving up Christianity these Tweenagers had in fact given up much more than they realised.

Two of the three negatives (being Rude and Unforgiving) worked in an exactly analogous but opposite way, with the highest percentage for those who were no longer Christian. Only one, that of Bully was different (with those of other religions having a higher percentage than for Christians).

There was one interesting denominational (or perhaps racial) variation for those who were Well-behaved – Pentecostal Tweenagers were much better at this than those from the New Churches (66% to 46%)!

Those who were regular churchgoers were much more likely to be Caring and Well-behaved than those who only went occasionally[6], whereas those who no longer went to church or never had been were much likely to be Daring, Lazy, Rude, Perfect and Unforgiving!

What then are the chief images which Tweenagers have of themselves? There are four which scored more than 60%:

- Five-sixths, 82%, see themselves as Friendly. This is their chief image; it is true of 90% of girls and 77% of boys. It does not vary with age. 86% of those who usually get A grades think of themselves as Friendly, against 73% who get C grades or lower.
- Two in 3, 67%, see themselves as Happy and about the same, 64%, as Funny. These percentages do not vary by age, gender, grades or Christian involvement.
- Overall five in every eight, 63%, see themselves as Caring, but this varies with gender – 76% of girls see themselves this way against only 50% of boys. 72% of those who usually get A grades think of themselves as Caring, against 53% who get C grades or lower. 69% of Christians see themselves as Caring, against 48% of those who are no longer Christian. 70% of those who go to church regularly see themselves as Caring, against 57% who only go occasionally and 56% who never go. The greatest of these variations relate to gender.

How would other Tweenagers describe you?

A selection of 13 answers was suggested, and again Tweenagers were allowed to tick all that they thought applied to them. On average nine were ticked across every two people. Overall replies are given in Table 9.2:

Table 9.2: How Tweenagers thought others saw them

Someone who is...	%	Someone who...	%
a good friend in time of trouble	75	is a boffin	16
a good laugh	73	gets into a lot of trouble	13
trustworthy	66	always wants their own way	10
a good person	66	is a nerd	6
knows what they are doing	46	is a bad person	3
a cool dude	37	doesn't care about others	3
a bit of a pain	27		

These answers reinforce the previous answers about image. Tweenagers see themselves as Friendly and assume others see themselves that way also. They wish to be seen as Funny and again this is reflected in the way they want others to see them as "a good laugh". This importance of fun is a key factor – church and youth programmes somehow need to build this, almost automatically, into everything they do for young people.

In the early 1990s, in an Anglican church where I was leading a vision building day, the vicar said he had four goals for the church. The fourth of these was simply the word "Fun". When I asked him what that meant, he replied, "I think to myself in everything we do, 'Where is the fun element in this?'". Precisely so! This question needs to become commonplace.

There are only three other descriptions which a reasonable proportion of Tweenagers wish others to see in them – someone you can trust, a good person and a confident person, someone who

knows what they are doing. As might be expected the various negative descriptions all receive low percentages, but that some know
others see themselves like this is again probably a realistic assessment.

None of these top five characteristics – Friendly, Fun,
Trustworthy, Good and Confident – varied by age of Tweenager.
Being Friendly did by gender, as it did with image, with 83% of girls
wanting themselves to be seen like this against 68% of boys. So did
being seen as "a good laugh", unlike the image of fun, with 79% of
girls wanting this and 69% of boys. Being trustworthy also varied
(76% girls to 58% boys), as did being good (72% girls and 61%
boys). All these variations had girls thinking others saw them that
way more than boys. Only being seen as confident did not vary by
gender. "Kids today are concerned about nothing so much as
appearing cool, unflustered"[7].

Being seen as a good friend varied by the grades usually
obtained. This was true of 80% who usually got As, 75% who got Bs
and 68% who got Cs or below. Likewise being seen as someone who
could be trusted was important for 72% who usually got As, 68%
who got Bs, and 54% who got Cs or below. (Did this perception
come from their academic confidence?) Being seen as someone who
knew what they were doing varied from 57% of those who usually
got As to 40% who got Bs and 43% who got Cs or below.

Nearly three-quarters, 71%, of those who were Christian wished
to be seen as a good person, against 62% of those who weren't sure,
53% of those who were no longer a Christian, 64% of those who had
never been a Christian, and 74% of those who belonged to another
religion. These variations indicate a critical component of how
Tweenagers view Christian and other religious people – they are
"good". Presumably this helps to explain why when they do something which they know isn't "good" they will tend to dissociate themselves from Christianity.

Likewise, four-fifths, 79%, of those who attend church regularly
wish to be seen as a good friend to have in trouble, against 67% who
attend occasionally, 81% who now never go, and 73% who have

never gone. The percentages for those who wish to be seen "as a good laugh" were, respectively, 70%, 74%, 82% and 76%, and for those who wanted to be seen as someone who could be trusted 72%, 60%, 70% and 65%. Those who have stopped going to church would like a higher image of themselves with respect to friendliness and fun. Does this give a clue as to why some of them had left church? They had not found friends there – perhaps there were no other young people their age – and they did not find church to be fun.

What this is saying is that to the images of being Friendly, Funny, Happy and Caring need to be added the desire to be seen as Trustworthy, Good and Confident. Gender and grades obtained will be the key determinants of these, not age or spiritual belief or activity. These seven traits focus on the need for a sense of community and deeper relationships, something not unique to British young people, as George Gallup has found among American youngsters[8].

Other supporting research

Leslie Francis has also researched the image of young people, using different statements from the above. Scottish young people aged 12 to 15 would affirm the self-confidence that emerges above as they strongly supported the statement "I feel my life has a sense of purpose" in a survey published in 2001[9]. English and Welsh adolescents found the same[10]. Another study found that sensitivity, boldness and cheerfulness were the top characteristics of 11 to 17 year olds[11].

A European survey found 74% of young people like "to meet friends"[12]. Five-sixths of American teenagers said "close friendships" were "very desirable"[13]. Happiness and religiosity are correlated[14]; 92% of American teenagers saw themselves as "happy" and 91% as "responsible"[15].

Part of the process is helping young people to decide "what is true", something that children and youth workers can often help with, described by Stephen Jones, an American pastor, as a "faith shaping task"[16]. A teenager whose parents had just divorced was confused as to what she should do. I simply asked her questions about how she weighed up different factors which enabled her to make her own mind up about her next steps; others can do likewise.

So what does all this mean?

This survey of Tweenagers has covered much ground. What has it said which may be helpful for church leadership as it seeks to reach and keep them?

1) Tweenagers herd together, and need to be reached that way

The Tweenagers that we have met through this survey, and face-to-face in Focus Groups, seek to be friendly to each other, and to "gang" together. They wish to work together, to relate, probably more strongly than previous generations of young people their age. This bunching together, going as a group, is to be encouraged if it can enable them all to stay longer in association with the church and the beliefs and lifestyle it teaches. This is where they feel secure, where their gang almost becomes family for them. It is also very hard for a Tweenager to "switch" to another group (with perhaps different values) even if s/he wishes[17].

Their high use of a mobile phone also enables them to band together, whether physically in the same place or not. It may not be accidental that the fastest growing church in the UK, the Kingsway International Christian Centre, targets Tweenagers by sending them text messages urging them to try church. The high usage of texting means that Tweenagers are developing their own language which church leaders at some stage will need to learn!

It may be necessary for those working with this group to use some of the methods used in cross-cultural evangelism in the third world when whole tribes or villages are sought to be won for Christ. These need to be studied further in this context, but it means identifying those who speak for the whole group, the mores by which decisions are made, and the group's values so that the best way of communicating the gospel may be made. Part of those mores are reflected in what Tweenagers said a good school was like... where beauty, comfort and safety were the top concerns.

2) Girls lead the boys

It used to be said that boys got girls into sexual trouble. While, from this study, it could be argued the reverse would seem more likely, it must be remembered that girls mature younger and are often seduced by older males, not their contemporaries. It is also true that more 14 year old girls have had sexual intercourse than boys the same age, but such male "experience" is not seen as getting girls into trouble. In terms of actually becoming pregnant (which is what the phrase originally meant), this happens fairly rarely compared to the number of times intercourse actually occurs, even though Britain has the highest teenage pregnancy rate in Europe.

The girls emerge as the more friendly, caring, thoughtful, hard-working, etc. They take the lead in many instances, in church as well as school. But they are also just as likely to leave Sunday School or church as boys.

We therefore need to focus especially on these girls. How do we help them accept the challenge of following Jesus, and exercise restraint and discipline? How do we help them persuade any boys in their 'gang' to do the same? How do we use their very positive desires for friendship, care and help in practical ways? Can we find ways of enabling them to be actively involved in projects of various kinds associated with the church, so that their Christianity has a practical and social dimension?

We need to focus on boys also, and maybe exercise positive discrimination toward them if they are feeling intimidated by high performing girls. Boys' clubs are one specific way perhaps of doing just this.

3) Reach Tweenagers while they are still children

Tweenagers decide for the church while they are still children, mostly when 7 to 10 years of age. They experience "church" in reality as Sunday School and their experience there so often makes or breaks their later participation in church, especially if it seems like "school". They may not leave while they are still in junior school, but a year or two into secondary school, then they leave – in droves. Perhaps three-quarters of 12 year olds in church will leave in their next two years.

Their Sunday School experience, especially while in the junior age-group is therefore critical. Unfortunately with many Sunday School teachers on rota, and both parents and children attending church irregularly, the opportunity of a real teacher-pupil relationship is rare. This is one reason why the Kids' Club in Liverpool is so successful – a small army of volunteers visits every child every week at home. Relational youth work is of paramount importance!

Another key reason is the falling percentage of those who respond to the Gospel message as they get older; the key age used to be in a person's teenage years, now it is in their childhood years.

4) We urgently need Child and Family Ministers in our churches

Youth Ministers are perhaps the most sought-after personnel in the church today, and imaginative ways of attracting them are used, as the advertisement[18] opposite testifies.

The basic numbers testify to the urgency of the problem – 1,000 children under 15 left the church in England *every week* during the 1990s. One thousand a week is 50,000 a year. 50,000 a year is half a million every decade. We only had 740,000 children in church in 1998, so it does not take a statistician to say we haven't much time left! This has been described as "close to panic in some quarters"[19].

We therefore **urgently** need a generation of Children's Workers or Child Ministers, just as we still desperately need Youth Ministers. Hopefully they can be recruited as enthusiastically and professionally as Youth Ministers are, not thwarted by the legal safeguards and requirements that now have to be gone through first.

It is crucial that churches have exceptionally good child protection policies in place in light of the scandals in the Catholic Church in North America in early 2002, and the earlier problems with the Canadian Anglican Church.

The editor of *YouthWork* believes the number of churches employing children's workers "will explode" during the first decade of the 21st century, because churches "will find it increasingly harder to recruit volunteers to oversee children's ministry"[20]. In 1998 the

Baptist Union reported 123 full-time youth specialists employed by local churches, but only 10 full-time children's specialists[21]; if all were employed by different churches that means 1 church in 15 had such a specialist.

Maybe Child Ministers need to be Child and Family Ministers, as the importance of stable home life is huge in shaping people's attitudes and actions. Tweenagers follow their parents' example. Encouraging regular church attendance will also help foster and deepen life values and a distinctive ethical behavioural stance[22] as well as Christian beliefs, as Robin Gill shows. However, "Family" may not be the right word as single parents and those who are cohabiting join the church. The correct word to use is "household" but a church can hardly appoint a "Child and Household" Minister!

Are parenting classes one way of helping parents think through their Christian responsibilities and opportunities? If parenting classes help reduce youth crime (as the BBC alleged[23]), could they encourage church and Christian involvement? And what about grandparenting classes?

5) The importance of grandparents

There are a number of places where grandparents come into the story (or the analysis). Sometimes they are seen as people of influence, either on their grandchildren directly or via their parents. Sometimes they are the "holders of the story" who reflect a practice to be followed when grandchildren visit[24]. Sometimes they are active in the development of their grandchildren, or in teaching Sunday School at their church. They can be especially important in helping their grandchildren's world to hold together if their parents divorce.

I suspect not enough attention has been paid to the grandparents' role and would wish to urge them to pray, act and encourage in every way possible the spiritual development of their grandchildren. How best this might be accomplished is not clear. Maybe just recognising the strategic role they often play will encourage some to keep going despite waning energy or increasing physical disability.

Could churches offer "foster grandparents" who could befriend young people and fulfil some of the roles the young people want? Churches are grey haired – it could be an asset! This is practised by some. Here is one situation (using aliases to protect identities):

Mary was born to parents who subsequently divorced. She stayed with her mother, while her father joined a household with two children. One of them, Tom, became Mary's very firm friend during her weekly visits on "Daddy's Day". Her grandfather kept in touch with his ex-son-in-law and now takes Tom to Sunday School most weeks, as well as taking out the two friends on other occasions. Who can tell where that kind of relationship will lead?

6) 'Fun' is a core value of Tweenagers

Fun cropped up again and again in the questionnaire results, and was the underlying theme in both Focus Groups (as also in the Scottish one). Yet church is not perceived as fun, and when asked what they would change to make church more attractive to young people their age, "Make it more fun" was a suggestion which met with the approval of most of those present. Apparently insignificant, "unspiritual" issues are the key ones for them – how they are talked to, can they have fun or make a noise, eat or do nothing in particular.

In another research project[25] an elderly Sunday School teacher observed that this generation of children "Don't want to be good, they want to be happy". For older generations of churchgoers, the idea of church being fun is a difficult concept and perhaps one of the main things they cannot understand about young people in church. How can church be made fun for young people – not only Tweenagers! – without denying the importance, and at times the seriousness, of the message we proclaim?

This means that note needs to taken for there to be "more interactive and participatory learning for children and an increasing sensitivity and awareness to the different learning styles of children"[26]. This could well mean meeting midweek rather than on Sunday, when "fun" can be introduced so much more easily.

Some fun can be creatively encouraged through an arts and music ministry. With so many young people learning to play music, church orchestras or bands can be stimulating, useful in encouraging talent, and actually fun for everyone – parents and grandparents alike!

7) The groups who aren't there regularly

This study has shown again and again that while there are Tweenagers who are in church, and likely to stay there, those who get grade As at school, there are equally many who only go occasionally, who are not sure if they are Christian, who get grade Bs or lower. These groups may be smaller in number than the first group in this study, but are likely much larger in the wider Tweenager world, and are vital for the future of the church, though they seem to be reached less effectively than the first group.

This is where alternative expressions of Christianity become so important – the Youth Service maybe, the Rock Solid or other Youth Clubs – and why every encouragement must be given to explore new and different ways of doing "church" with them. In the five year vision which Crusaders have produced "reaching" and "engaging" young people are its two top challenges[27]. The implications of reaching the many Tweenagers who regularly get grade B or less are huge for a largely middle class church, who must either see their culture changed or alternative "churches" spring up outside their structures.

In practice this means finding alternative ways in which young people can worship and serve togther, both elements being important. Having "fun" is a critical part of this process, as noted above, without which such efforts will fail. We also need to learn how Tweenagers define fun; it may not be as adults think it should be! It will almost certainly include electronic games!

There are simply too many Tweenagers on the edge for them to be left out of future considerations of church, and as they grow older will hopefully help transform the existing church into a format which will attract many more Mosaics. Part of that attraction will be the use of more modern teaching methods – young people used to

Powerpoint presentations at school often find church methods dated, and unfortunately can associate that image with the message.

8) There is an ignorance of "church" and Christian values

Many Tweenagers have no idea what "church" is like. One of the questions raised in a Children's Work forum was precisely this[28]. Some Tweenagers have only been to a church because of a christening, wedding or funeral. They do not know what "worship" means. Yet they will say they are "spiritual", and many engage in "religious" exercises like praying, or occasionally reading the Bible. Many Tweenagers have been baptised as infants. Many think about God and picture him as Creator, Father and Friend. A quarter have had what they call a "religious experience", and half knew someone who had had such.

Honesty is a critical component of Tweenagers' value systems. The first two years at secondary school are crucial for a reappraisal of their values, and they may well then discard some by which they have hitherto lived and take on new ones. Is there some way in which these changes and spiritual values can be intertwined? Confidence in spiritual things is linked with confidence in other areas of a Tweenager's life.

People outside their close family and friends are only trusted if they know them. They also know which teachers they will listen to. Churches need to create opportunities to build relationships with Tweenagers which allow trust to develop. They also need to ensure that anyone who teaches the Tweenagers they already have is able to do so in such a way that the youngsters will listen.

Tweenagers are not certain Christianity is relevant for them. The crux revolves around the person of Jesus Christ. Is He really the Son of God, or was He an ordinary man? Did He really exist? We have come full circle. Help Tweenagers understand who Jesus is (and other doctrines), and they then hopefully will understand the church better and appreciate the Christian lifestyle and values – and may even follow them! Let's hope so – for the sake of the Kingdom!

9) Tweenagers throughout the UK are similar

Although this project and the Scottish survey of 11 to 14s each had only one Focus Group among churchgoing Tweenagers, the findings are almost identical. This not only validates the results from each survey but also shows that geographical location or the variety in the church scene in different parts of the UK does not radically affect the attitudes and values of this age-group (though Scottish Tweenagers are not, or at least not yet, leaving the church in such large proportions as their English counterparts[29]).

The work of Leslie Francis also shows comparatively small differences between secondary school age young people across Britain. This means that, while this research was carried out exclusively in England, its findings and proposals are applicable elsewhere.

NOTES

[1] As in *Time* magazine, 18th March, 2002, Page 93.

[2] Details in Table A4/41 in Appendix 4.

[3] Details in Table A4/42 in Appendix 4.

[4] Details in Table A4/45 in Appendix 4.

[5] Details in Table A4/43 in Appendix 4.

[6] Details in Table A4/44 in Appendix 4.

[7] Article "The blank generation" by Ruth Mittens in *The Leading Light,* Volume 2, Number 1, Winter 1995, Page 19.

[8] *The Spiritual Life of Young Americans approaching the year 2000,* George H Gallup, Jnr, The George H Gallup International Institute, Princeton, New Jersey, United States, 1995, Page 101.

[9] Article "God images and self-worth among adolescents in Scotland" by Leslie Francis, Harry Gibson and Mandy Robbins in *Mental Health, Religion and Culture,* Volume 4, Number 2, November 2001, Page 106.

[10] Chapter "The social significance of religious affiliation among adolescents [13 to 15 year olds] in England and Wales" by Leslie Francis in *Religious Individualization and Christian Religious Semantics* by Hans-George Ziebertz et al, Lit Verlag, 2001, Page 115.

[11] Article "Comparing Cattell's personality factors and Eysenck's personality dimensions among adolescents" by Rosamund Bourke and Leslie Francis in *The Irish Journal of Psychology,* Volume 21, Number 1/2, 2000, Page 99.

[12] *Young people on the threshold of the year 2000,* A Eurobarometer survey, Education Training Youth, European Commission, Luxembourg, 1997, Page 9.

[13] Article "Teenagers and the Future" by George Barna in *The Barna Report,* April–June 1999, Page 6.

[14] Article "Religiosity and Happiness: During Adolescence, Young Adulthood and later Life" by Leslie Francis, Susan Jones and Carolyn Wilcox, *Journal of Psychology and Christianity,* Volume 19, Number 3, 2000, Page 245.

[15] *Third Millennium Teens,* George Barna Report, Barna Research Group, Ventura, California, 1999, Page 8.

[16] *What characterises adolescents in the contemporary world and what possible Christian responses are there?,* a paper written by Nigel James, Field Officer, Boys' Brigade in Wales, 1993, Page 20.

[17] Part of a presentation by Murray Milner on *"The Implicit Religion of American Teenagers"* at the Denton Conference of the Network for the Study of Implicit Religion, May 2001.

[18] Reproduced, with permission, from Rev Peter Hywell-Jones, Boldmere, West Midlands.

[19] *Producing a Strategy for children and young people's work,* Rev Philip Mounstephen, CPAS, Mini-Guide 18, Administry, Sheffield, September 2001, Page 1.

[20] Personal letter from John Buckeridge, 4th April 2002.

[21] Report from their 1998 annual returns by Rev Darrell Jackson, Mission Adviser, August 2000.

[22] See, for example, Philip Mounstephen's *Search Engine,* CPAS, 2001, which is designed to help Tweenagers develop a Christian world view which will sustain them in their Christian commitment and behaviour.

[23] Item on the BBC1 6.00 pm News programme, 10 July 2002.

[24] Cp article "Telling our children the story" by Dwight Longenecker, *Priests & People,* London, December 2001, Page 455.

[25] *The SALT Users' Survey,* a large Christian Research project for Scripture Union, Bletchley, 1998, included both quantitative surveys and qualitative Focus Groups.

[26] Article "Children... Today's Church, as well as Tomorrow's", *Netfax,* Leadership Network, Number 59, 25 November 1996, Page 1.

[27] *A Vision for Youth,* Crusaders 5 Year Strategy Overview, Matt Summerfield, 2001, Page 3.

[28] The *Children's Work Forum,* addressing issues related to 8–11 year olds, was held at High Leigh Conference Centre in February 2001, facilitated by Heather Wraight of Christian Research, using as its base a pre-circulated paper by Penny Frank of CPAS.

[29] One finding from the results of the 2002 Scottish Church Census, to be published in 2003. Contact Christian Research for details.

[30] Based on those in *The Oxford Statement on Children at Risk,* produced at the January 1997 Consultation facilitated by the Viva Network and the Oxford Centre for Mission Studies, Oxford.

Postscript

It is right to concentrate on the situation in the UK, and to think through how children can be helped into the Kingdom of God. There is a place to gather relevant data, discuss it, and think through its strategic implications. But there is a wider world, where needs are very different from those in the UK, which shouts for attention also. In a book which looks only at the West, and the decline of young people in the church, one needs to reflect also on the following statistics[30] as a way of painting that larger scene as the needs of these children are no less desperate:

Number of children (under 15) in the world in 2002:	1,200,000,000
Number conceived each year:	160,000,000
Number aborted each year:	40,000,000
Number actually born each year:	120,000,000
Number living on the streets:	100,000,000
Number in forced prostitution:	10,000,000
Number made to join prostitution each year:	1,000,000
Average length of time as a prostitute:	10 years
Number dying of malnutrition each year:	13,000,000
Number dying for lack of immunisation each year:	2,000,000
Number losing their home because of war each year:	1,200,000
Number killed each year:	150,000
Number disabled or maimed each year:	400,000
Number in slavery or child labour:	150,000,000
Number infected with AIDS:	1,500,000
Number going blind each year:	500,000
Number committing suicide each year:	?100,000

If our Tweenagers can be transformed by a relationship with Jesus Christ, they may be the key to reducing these appalling figures in 10 or 20 years time.

Appendix 1:
Sponsors and Council of Reference

We are extremely grateful that this research has been supported and advised by so many. The survey sponsors, by finance or in kind, were:

The Baptist Union of Great Britain
The Boys' Brigade
The Church Army
Church Pastoral Aid Society
Crusaders
Evangelical Alliance
J W Laing Trust
Salesians of Don Bosco
Spring Harvest
Youth for Christ

Likewise we are very grateful for those who gave many hours serving on the Steering Committee, to help guide the entire project.

Richard Bromley (Chair)	Youth for Christ
Darrell Jackson (initially)	Baptist Union of Great Britain
Nick Lear (later)	Baptist Union of Great Britain
Capt Ron Davies	Church Army
Rev Philip Mounstephen	Church Pastoral Aid Society
Matt Summerfield	Crusaders
Ishmael Smale (initially)	Evangelical Alliance
Danny Brierley (later)	Evangelical Alliance
Martin Poulsom	Salesians of Don Bosco
Rachael Orrell	Spring Harvest

Those who have been kind enough to comment on an initial draft of this manuscript were:

Richard Bromley	Youth For Christ
John Buckeridge	Youthwork
Revd Anthony Burnham	Moderator, Free Churches Group
The Revd Gill Dallow	Diocese of Leicester
Sydney Jones OBE	Boys' Brigade
Penny Frank	Church Pastoral Aid Society
Nick Lear	Baptist Union of Great Britain
John Marshall	formerly Director of Ministry, Saltmine
Revd Philip Mounstephen	Church Pastoral Aid Society
Martin Poulsom	Salesians of Don Bosco
Debby Sharp	Northamptonshire Association of Youth Clubs
Heather Wraight	Christian Research

Appendix 2: Methodology

Quantitative research

This carefully planned survey was aimed at four groups of Tweenagers:

- Those who currently go to church on Sunday, but distinguishing between different types of frequency
- Those who are involved with a Christian activity (like Boys' Brigade, church youth club, Crusaders, etc) during the week but who do not go to church on Sunday
- Those who do not go to church at all, contacted via schools
- Those who had stopped going to church, by far the most difficult group to contact.

A questionnaire was sent to a carefully selected random probability sample of ministers, taking into account such factors as denomination, churchmanship, church environment and geographical location. Each participating church was sent an appropriate number of forms, up to a maximum of 20. A total of 1,008 ministers across four denominations were chosen and asked if they would distribute forms to children in their church aged between 10 and 14. One in every eight, 12% [123 churches], agreed to do so.

The number of forms requested is shown in the Table on the next page, together with the number of responding churches to whom they were sent. No church was sent more than 20 forms, however many were requested. It is not possible to know if all the forms sent were distributed, but if they were, the response rate was 38% [549 forms]. If fewer were actually distributed, the response rate would be proportionately higher.

Table A2/1: Number of forms sent to which types of church

		Evangelical				Non-evangelical				Total
		Ang	*Bap*	*Meth*	*New*	*Ang*	*Bap*	*Meth*	*New*	
N	City	5/1	8/1	15/1	0/0	0/0	0/0	0/0	0/0	28/3
O	Sub	68/7	8/1	8/1	20/2	135/10	0/0	18/2	88/5	345/28
R	Town	20/2	18/2	0/0	0/0	22/3	0/0	0/0	0/0	60/7
T										
H	Rural	48/4	0/0	0/0	0/0	62/4	0/0	0/0	30/2	140/10
S	City	10/1	28/2	19/2	0/0	8/1	8/1	0/0	0/0	73/7
O	Sub	94/11	68/3	0/0	0/0	184/13	28/2	6/1	14/1	394/31
U										
T	Town	144/8	42/3	6/1	16/2	77/8	0/0	0/0	30/2	315/24
H	Rural	24/3	16/2	0/0	0/0	58/7	8/1	0/0	0/0	106/13
	Total	**413/37**	**188/14**	**48/5**	**36/4**	**546/46**	**44/4**	**24/3**	**162/10**	**1,461/123**

The first figure is the number of forms sent, the second the number of churches

Christian youth organisations, especially those represented on the Steering Committee, were asked if they would distribute forms to their classes, groups, clubs etc. All kindly did so. We are especially grateful to the Boys' Brigade and the Church Army for asking young people whom they knew had stopped going to church to complete a form. It is impossible to know exactly how many forms were actually distributed, probably far fewer than the 1,580 supplied. 327 were returned, a notional response rate of 21%, but most likely probably the real response was nearer twice or even three times that.

A selection of 77 schools in the same areas as participating churches were also approached to ask if a form could be completed by relevant classes. The school year for class distribution varied from Year 6 in primary schools to Years 7 to 10 in secondary schools. Two-thirds of the schools were willing to help, and although again the exact number of forms distributed is not known, 63% of those sent were returned [1,296 forms], suggesting a rather higher rate of response since not every school would have distributed all the forms. Seven of the schools were suggested by the Association of Christian Teachers, and there were 10 Church of England schools and 10 Catholic secondary schools in the numbers approached.

The questionnaire was subject to extensive testing, with a pilot, and advice from a Diocesan Children's Officer.

Attitudinal Research

Qualitative or attitudinal research was undertaken by means of two Discussion or Focus Groups, with young people of this age range, one in a church context and one in a non-church.

Desk Research

In addition to the above, desk research was also undertaken with a review of the literature and other religious research carried out. Extracts from the findings of others who have undertaken research among this age group have been incorporated with the text throughout.

The Report

The actual questionnaire used is given in Appendix 3, together with percentages to the answer to each question. These have been analysed and reported as follows:

Chapter 1: Questions 1–3 and 17
Chapter 2: Questions 13–15 and 18
Chapter 3: None
Chapter 4: Questions 4–7
Chapter 5: Questions 8 and 30
Chapter 6: Questions 19–29
Chapter 7: Questions 9–11 and 16
Chapter 8: Questions 31 to 37
Chapter 9: Question 12.

The result is this book of 57,500 words, excluding 6,000 in the Appendices.

Appendix 3

EARLY AND PRE-TEENS SURVEY

What is this survey? It looks at how young people spend their spare time and what they think about religion and the church.
Who should complete it? Young people aged between 10 and 14 years old. All your answers are confidential and no one else at your school or church will read them.
What should I do?　1) Do not write your name on the questionnaire
　　　　　　　　　　2) Please tick ☑ only <u>one answer for each question</u> unless it asks you to tick more than one.
　　　　　　　　　　3) When you have finished put it in the envelope you have been given and seal it. Give it back to your leader/teacher.　Thank you for your help.

YOU AND THE THINGS YOU THINK AND DO

1. What school year are you in?

5 Year 5 or below	23 Year 8	2 Year 11 or
12 Year 6	22 Year 9	above
21 Year 7	15 Year 10	

2. Are you:

47 A boy　　　　　　53 A girl

3. What grades do you mostly get for your school/college work?
(Please tick one box only)

30 A	12 C	1 E & F
45 B	2 D	10 Not graded

4. What sort of television programmes do you watch?(Please tick all that apply)

24 Animal/nature	44 Game shows
58 Cartoons	9 Information
81 Comedy	25 News
14 Cookery	37 Quiz shows
7 Current affairs	7 Religious programmes
20 Documentaries	67 Soaps
6 Discussion	47 Sport/leisure
23 DIY/gardening	4 Don't watch much
79 Films	television

5. Do you own any of the following yourself? (Please tick all that apply)

74 Computer	66 Personal Stereo
22 DVD	4 Playnet
62 Mobile phone	35 Televideo
80 Music system	61 TV in your room
61 Personal CD	36 Video in your room
61 Playstation/Dreamcast/N64	10 WAP phone

6. Do you have your own room?

84 Yes, all to myself　　　16 No, I share with
　　　　　　　　　　　　　brothers/sisters

7a. Do you have access to a computer?

94 Yes　　　　　　6 No (go to Q8)

7b. If yes, do you have access to the Internet?

81 Yes　　　　　　13 No (go to Q8)

7c. If yes, how often do you access the Internet?

9 More than once a day	9 Once a month
24 Once a day	9 Less than once a month
30 Once a week	

7d. What do you use the Internet for?(Please tick all that apply)

27 Chat rooms	8 News	13 Shopping
55 E-mails	45 Play games	14 Other (please specify)
55 Information	33 Play music	_____

8. What else do you do in your spare time? (Please tick one box per row)

	I do it: on my own	with friends	with other people	I don't do it
Do homework	84	6	5	5
Go to church activities	4	28	17	51
Go to discos/nightclubs	1	60	7	32
Go to the cinema	2	77	15	6
Go to a youth/church club	4	39	9	48
Hang around with friends	4	88	3	5
Listen to music	67	26	4	3
Play arcade games	13	36	6	45
Play home computer/ electronic games	59	25	7	9
Play team sports	3	57	23	17
Read books and comics	77	4	1	18
Skate/rollerblade/cycle	21	52	9	18
Spend time with boyfriend or girlfriend	25	19	2	54
Watch videos/DVD	25	52	17	6
Watch television	50	27	21	2
Other hobbies/interests (please specify)_____	23	45	14	18

9. For each of the following statements please indicate whether you agree or disagree: (please tick one box per row)

	Agree	Not sure	Disagree
Everyone needs a hero in their life	29	41	30
In times of trouble or crisis I feel all alone	36	28	36
It is always wrong to tell lies	42	28	30
It is always wrong to cheat	67	19	14
It is better to get even than mad	38	36	26
It is OK to copy things from other people if you are in a hurry	24	31	45
It is OK to take little things like pencils from school	12	17	71
Life's too short to worry	43	28	29
My opinions and attitudes are not taken seriously	27	42	31
One person cannot really make a difference in this world	22	23	55
Sometimes it is necessary to tell a lie	66	21	13
Stealing is always wrong	73	15	12
The future will be better than today	25	61	14
The main purpose of life is enjoyment and personal fulfilment	55	30	15
There is no one who I consider to be my hero or role model	28	31	41

Keep going, you're doing fine!!!

10. Do you do any activity that helps other people around where you live? (Please tick all that apply)

22 Yes, on my own   33 Yes, through my school
19 Yes, through church   38 No
18 Yes, through other groups like Scouts/Guides

11a. If you found a £20 note lying on the pavement, would you: (Please tick one only)

5 Leave it there
24 Pick it up and hand it in at the police station
58 Pick it up and keep it
13 Pick it up and give it to charity

11b. If you found two £50 notes lying on the pavement, would you: (Please tick one only)

3 Leave them there
42 Pick them up and hand them in at the police station
40 Pick them up and keep them
8 Pick them up and give them to charity
7 Pick one up and leave the other

12a. What sort of person do you think you are? (Please tick all that apply)

14 Angry	57 Helpful	57 Reliable
24 Annoying	36 Lazy	14 Rude
20 Bossy	23 Leader	11 Scared
3 Bully	45 Mature	7 Self-centred
63 Caring	41 Messy 27 Shy	
36 Daring	28 Moody	9 Slow
35 Forgetful	43 Noisy	52 Sporty
82 Friendly	24 Ordinary	57 Talkative
64 Funny	21 Quiet	54 Thoughtful
20 Fussy	15 Peaceful	7 Unforgiving
67 Happy	10 Perfect	26 Unusual
56 Hard-working	49 Playful	48 Well-behaved

12b. How do you think other people would describe you? (Please tick all that apply)

75 A good friend to have when there is trouble	3 A bad person
	73 A good laugh
13 Someone who gets into a lot of trouble	16 A boffin
	37 A cool dude
46 Someone who knows what they are doing	6 A nerd
	66 Someone you can trust
3 Someone who doesn't care about others	27 A bit of a pain
	66 A good person
10 Someone who always wants their own way	

13. Which of the following do you trust? (Please tick all that apply)

89 Parents	5 Politicians
71 Other family members	7 People on Television
56 Police	3 People who write in newspapers
44 Teachers	
17 Social workers	14 Lawyers
59 Doctors and nurses	34 Other children and young people
31 People who go to church	
42 Church leaders(vicar/minister)	35 Childline
32 Youth club leaders	29 A neighbour
19 Leaders of things like guides/scouts	

14. Which one of the following statements comes closest to describing how you would define a family? (Please tick one box only)

37 Where all members of the family are related to each other by birth, adoption or marriage
56 Any person or group whom you love or care about deeply, or who love or care about you deeply
4 Any group of people who live in the same home together
3 Any group of people who share the same set of values and goals in life

15. Which of the following statements best describes your home? My home is a place where... (Please tick one box only)

59 I feel secure and loved
9 Each of us is trying to love each other
24 Sometimes I feel loved, other times I don't
4 I usually feel uncomfortable and would rather be elsewhere
4 I feel comfortable, although we are not a close, loving family

16. Over the past three months have you done any of the following activities (remember, everything you tell us is anonymous and confidential): (Please tick all that apply)

69 Watched a horror or violent film
6 Used an illegal drug
15 Cheated on an exam or test
7 Stolen money
5 Been involved in shoplifting

56 Lied to a parent, teacher or other adult
46 Lied to a friend or another young person
20 Drank enough alcohol to get drunk
17 Intentionally tried to hurt someone physically
20 Intentionally tried to hurt someone's feelings
13 Smoked a cigarette

WHAT YOU THINK ABOUT RELIGION AND CHURCH

17. Which of the following statements best describes your present religious commitment? (Please tick one box only)

55 I am a Christian
24 I am not sure if I am a Christian
3 I am no longer a Christian
14 I have never been a Christian
4 I belong to another religion (please specify)

* If you belong to another religion, then wherever you see the word "church" please think of "temple" or "mosque" or the place you usually go to for worship if you can, but if you can't then please go to the next question.

18. Do you know if your parents and grandparents have ever gone to church? (Please tick one box for each column)

	Parents	Grandparents (Mum's Parents)	(Dad's Parents)
No, they have never gone	13	10	13
They go occasionally	19	22	18
They used to go regularly but they don't go now	12	13	10
They have recently started going to church	2	1	1
One goes to church but the other does not	12	6	5
They have always gone regularly	29	24	23
I don't know	13	24	31

19. Do you now, or have you ever gone to church or Sunday school on a Sunday? (Please tick one only)

24 No, I have never been (go to Q26)
22 No, I used to go but I don't go now (go to Q20a)
18 Yes, I go occasionally (go to Q21)
36 Yes, I go regularly (go to Q22)

20a. If you stopped going to a church, Sunday school or junior church, how old were you when you stopped going?

20b. Why did you stop going? (Please tick all that apply)

7 Family pressure	44 I grew out of it
4 I started going to see the parent that I don't live with	46 I did not enjoy it
10 My friends stopped going	23 There were few other people there of my age
18 There were no activities for young people	4 I was always late
	11 Moved out of the area
7 Did not get on with the leaders	7 I didn't like the way I was treated
9 Did not get on with other young people /children	3 The services were too lively
12 I had serious doubts about the Christian religion	17 Church services started too early
37 The worship service was boring	
12 Did not understand the services	8 The congregation was not welcoming
23 The services were old-fashioned	
18 Some other reason (please specify)_____	

Now go to Q24

21. If you go to church occasionally, what sorts of things do you go to church for? (Please tick all that apply)

18 Confirmation	20 Youth service
62 Wedding/ funeral	17 Church parade
49 Christening/baptism/dedication	34 Easter Day
34 Carol service	24 Harvest Festival
38 Christmas day /midnight mass	23 Mothering Sunday
24 Something else (please specify)_____	

Now go to Q24

22. Can you remember why you started going to church? (Please tick one only) *If you go to more than one church, please answer the questions for the church you go to most often.*

65 My parents took me to church as a baby because they go there
4 My parents sent me to Sunday School but did not go to church themselves
1 My family moved nearby and came from another church
5 I first went to church through a church activity

3 I was curious about what went on there
3 I first went with my grandparents
5 My friends go and asked me to go too
6 Another reason (please specify)_____
8 Don't know

23. What is it about the church that you go to that you most like? (Please tick all that apply)

23 Bible teaching	29 Youth leaders
28 Strong presence of God	20 Youth worship
45 Caring people	19 The minister
34 Enjoyable music	32 Helps(ed) me worship God
41 Enjoyable Sunday youth group	25 Enjoyable drama
22 Enjoyable mid-week activities activities	27 Enjoyable social
51 Opportunity to meet friends/ new people	28 It is where I have always gone
7 Other (please specify)_____	13 Not sure

24. How old were you when you started going to church?

25. What kind of church do you or did you go to? (Please tick one only)(If you go to more than one church please think about the church you go to most often)

48 Church of England	2 Independent
6 Roman Catholic	2 House/New Church
10 Baptist	9 Methodist
2 Pentecostal	8 Other (please specify)
13 Don't know	

26. Many young people your age do not go to church, and others have stopped going. Why do you think that is? (Please tick all that you think apply)

87 They think it is boring	39 They think it is irrelevant
64 They don't believe in God	61 None of their friends go
17 They don't feel welcome	33 They feel out of place
16 Their families have moved away	67 They can't be bothered
18 They go out with their parents	11 They go out with their grandparents
43 They have never thought about it	
23 They don't like the people who do go	14 They don't like the minister/ leader
41 They don't know anyone at church	22 They don't like the moral teaching
34 They don't know what happens at church	73 They think going to church isn't cool
63 They've got other things to do on a Sunday	48 Their parents don't encourage them to go
49 They don't get up early enough on Sundays to go to church	15 Their parents might not like the minister/vicar
23 They go to see the parent that they don't live with	
6 Another reason (please specify)_____	

27. Why do you think some young people go to church? (Please tick all that apply)

68 They have always gone	53 Their parents send them
60 They enjoy it	17 It's near home
41 Because they think they should	57 Their parents/family go
64 To learn about God and Jesus	38 To meet their friends
24 To sing hymns	24 To get points for their church youth activity
6 Some other reason (please specify)_____	

28. How often do you do each of the following activities: (please tick one box per row)

	Daily	Weekly	Monthly	Occasionally	Never
Read part of the Bible	9	18	4	31	38
Pray to God	32	14	4	24	26
Attend a church based youth group	2	37	4	9	48
Lead a church based youth group	1	3	1	6	89
Take an active part in church services	2	12	10	28	48
Attend a Bible study group	2	9	2	7	80

29a. Would you tell your friends if you went to church or to a youth activity based in a church?

48 Yes   20 No   32 Maybe

Hang on in there, nearly finished now!!

29b. What do you think your friends and other people would say if they thought that you went to a church or a youth activity based in a church? (Please tick one only)

16 They might be curious and ask me questions
32 They might make fun of me or think I am stupid or uncool
6 I would be too shy to tell anyone
3 They belong to another religion so they would not be bothered
33 I have already told my friends that I go
10 Something else (please specify)_____

30a. Do you regularly attend any of the following activities in a church hall during the week? (Please tick all that apply)

5 Boys/Girls Brigade	14 Out of school clubs
6 Campaigners/Crusaders/ Pathfinders	9 Holiday clubs
4 Rock Solid Clubs	13 Scouts/Guides
20 Sunday school/junior church	19 Youth Club
19 Youth group/fellowship	12 Drama/Music group
34 No (go to Q31a)	4 Other (please specify) _____

30b. Would you describe these activities as:

31 Excellent	5 Poor	13 Average
45 Good	6 Don't know	

YOUR BELIEFS AND EXPERIENCES

31a. Which of the following do you believe in? (Please tick all that apply)

72 God	50 Hell	28 Re-incarnation
73 Heaven	67 Jesus	43 The Devil

31b. What do you think happens to people when they die? (Please tick one box only)

19 Everyone goes to heaven
35 Good people go to heaven and bad people go to hell
13 Only Christians go to heaven
10 People die and are born again as someone else
8 People die and are born again as another creature
15 Nothing, everything just stops

31c. Do you ever think about whether or not God exists?

58 Yes	24 No	18 Not sure

31d. Do you believe that you can have a relationship with God?

45 Yes	25 No	30 Not sure

32. Which of the following come into your picture of God? (Please tick all that apply)

62 Creator	48 Love	5 Policeman
57 Father	9 Mother	35 Saviour
22 Judge	35 Old man	4 Spoilsport
53 Friend	9 Other (please specify)_____	

33. Who do you think Jesus Christ is/was? (Please tick one only)

13 A very wise person   68 The son of God
8 An ordinary person   11 Someone who never existed

34. In your opinion what makes a person a Christian? (Please tick all that apply)

28 Being born in a Christian family	14 Going to a Christian school
49 Being baptised/ Christened	
3 Being born in the UK	42 Knowing Jesus as a personal saviour
66 Believing in God	
49 Believing the Bible is true	26 Leading a good life
36 Going to church	7 Don't know
21 Saying that they are Christian	
3 Something else (please specify)_____	

35. Have you been: (Please tick all that apply)

40 Baptised	55 Christened
19 Admitted to communion	16 Confirmed
15 Admitted to membership of a church	

36a. Have you ever experienced any of these? (Please tick one box per row)

	Yes	Not sure	No
An experience of becoming a Christian	35	29	36
A healing experience	15	25	60
Visions/voices/strange dreams	38	17	45
Something beyond description	23	22	55
Feeling as if somebody/something were trying to communicate with you	31	24	45
A feeling of peace during a church service	38	20	42
An experience to do with nature	22	28	50
The presence of God	32	26	42
Some other spiritual/supernatural force	20	26	54
Something else (please specify)	7	11	82

36b. Do you know any other people who have had experiences like these?

47 Yes	53 No (go to Q37)

36c. If yes, what do you think about them or their experience? (Please tick one only)

42 I can relate to them/it	15 It sounds scary
7 I'm envious	14 I think they are a bit mad
5 It was a coincidence	
17 Other (please specify) _____	

37. Do you think that Christianity is relevant to you?

52 Yes	21 No	27 Not sure

Well done - you're a star!!

Thank you very much. Now please put the questionnaire in the envelope provided and hand it back to your teacher or group leader.

Appendix 4: Extra Tables

Table A4/1: Grades mostly obtained at school by age (Page 5)
(Question 1 x Question 3)

Age in years	A %	B %	C %	D–F %
10	30	57	10	3
11	35	55	10	0
12	37	50	11	2
13	34	51	13	2
14	28	44	23	5
Overall	34	51	13	2

Table A4/2: Grades mostly obtained at school by gender (Page 6)
(Question 2 x Question 3)

Gender	A %	B %	C %	D–F %
Boy	29	52	16	3
Girl	38	51	10	1
Overall	34	51	13	2

Table A4/3: Tweenagers' churchgoing habits and parental churchgoing (Page 39)
(Question 18 x Question 19)

| Parental churchgoing frequency | Tweenager's churchgoing | | | | Overall |
	Regular %	Occasional %	Lapsed %	Never %	%
Regular	65	16	9	4	33
Occasional	8	42	28	26	22
Lapsed	4	14	33	16	14
Never	2	8	17	51	15
One parent only	19	18	12	2	14
Recently started	2	2	1	1	2
Base	672	303	333	283	1,591

This Table shows that **parental practice is followed by their children.** So two-thirds, 65%, of Tweenagers who go regularly have parents who have always gone to church. (Two-fifths, 42%, of occasional Tweenage churchgoers have parents who go to church occasionally. A third, 33%, of Tweenagers who have stopped going to church have parents who have done the same (did they all stop together?), and almost the same proportion, 28%, have parents who go only occasionally. Half, 51%, the Tweenagers who have never been to church have parents who have never been either.

Table A4/4: Churchgoing habits of parents by Tweenager's religious commitment
(Page 39)

| Parental churchgoing frequency | Tweenager's religious commitment | | | | | Overall |
	Certain %	Unsure %	Lapsed %	Never %	Other faith %	%
Regular	46	23	4	3	25	33
Occasional	20	29	20	16	35	22
Lapsed	11	18	27	18	9	14
Never	6	13	27	59	18	15
One parent only	16	16	20	3	10	14
Recently started	1	1	2	1	3	2
Base	1,015	432	44	243	75	1,089

Both in Table A4/3 and Table A4/4 the highlighted cells show where the figures are especially different from the overall percentage. Table A4/4 shows:

- Almost half, 46%, of Christian Tweenagers are in homes where their parents attend church regularly, and a further fifth, 20%, where their parents go occasionally.
- Almost a third, 29%, of Tweenagers who aren't sure if they are Christian have parents who attend church only occasionally, with a further quarter, 23%, having regularly attending parents.

- Over a half collectively, 54%, of Tweenagers who no longer consider themselves Christian have parents who have either never gone to church or who no longer attend. Was it just too hard for them?
- Three-fifths, 59%, of Tweenagers who have never been a Christian have parents who have never gone to church, with a further sixth, 18%, who no longer go.
- Three-fifths, 60%, of Tweenagers who belong to another religion have parents who either attend their place of worship regularly or occasionally.

Table A4/5: Religious commitment by parental churchgoing habits (Page 39)
(Questions 17 and 18)

Parental	Tweenager's religious commitment					
churchgoing	Certain	Unsure	Lapsed	Never	Other faith	**Base**
frequency	%	%	%	%	%	
Regular	80	15	1	1	3	748
Occasional	54	29	2	8	7	346
Lapsed	48	30	5	15	2	224
Never	27	20	5	43	5	238
One parent only	66	25	4	2	3	228
Recently started	56	24	4	8	8	25
Overall	55	24	14	3	4	1,089

This Table shows:

- Four-fifths, 80%, of parents who go to church regularly have Tweenager children who say they are Christian, and a further 15% who are not sure. For occasional parental churchgoers, just over half, 54%, of their children say they are Christian, with a further third, 29%, uncertain.
- Three children in seven, 43%, of children of parents who have never gone to church say they have never been a Christian, but, interestingly, a quarter, 27%, of non-churchgoing parents have children who say they are Christian.

- Half, 48%, of the Tweenager children of parents who have given up churchgoing say they are Christian, and a further third, 30%, are uncertain. One in seven, 15%, have never been Christian.

- Two-thirds, 66%, of children of couples where parental behaviour is split, one partner going to church and the other not, will say they are Christian, and a further quarter, 25% are unsure.

- A small number of parents in this sample of Tweenagers had recently started going to church. The majority, 56%, of these had Tweenagers who were Christian. Did their example help the parents start going to church?

Table A4/6:
Churchgoing habits of paternal grandparents and Tweenager's churchgoing (Page 41)
(Questions 17 and 18)

Paternal grandparents' churchgoing frequency	Tweenager's churchgoing				Base
	Regular %	Occasional %	Lapsed %	Never %	
Regular	60	16	15	9	391
Occasional	36	18	22	24	313
Lapsed	32	23	26	19	179
Never	24	17	24	35	211
One parent only	48	22	18	12	82
Recently started	48	16	12	24	25
Overall	36	18	22	24	**1,201**

Table A4/7: Other activities undertaken in Tweenager's spare time (Page 79)
(detail from Table 5.2)

Among indoor activities:

- *Musical instruments* included: Piano (25), Flute (16), Clarinet (8), Violin (7), Brass band (6), Guitar (6), Bell ringing (5), Cello (4), Drum (4), Jazz (3), Double bass (1), Oboe (1), Organ (1), Saxophone (1) and Tenor horn (1).

- *Inside hobbies* included: Computer/web (6), Writing stories (6), Needlework (and cross stitch and French knitting) (5), Reading (3), Cooking (2), Magic (2), Watching TV/Videos (2), Clothes design (1), Hair design (1), Joinery (1), Juggling (1), Pottery (1) and Puppet theatre (1).
- *Games* included: Bowling (8), Snooker or pool (8), Badminton (3), Table tennis (3), Card games (1), Chess (1), Darts (1), Pokemon cards (1) and Skipping (1).
- Arts and craft included drawing and painting.
- *Model making* included: Airfix models (3).
- *Relationships* included: Spending time with family (9), Talking to friends (including phoning) (7), Fighting (3!) and Parties (2).
- *Collecting things* included: Stamps (4), Books (2), Beer mats (1), Coins (1), John Deere (1), Gems (1), Models (1) and Super heroes (1).
- *Spiritual activities* included: Bible study (1), Church (1), Occult (1) and Prayer (1).

Among outdoor activities:

- *Other Sport,* that is, apart from soccer and tennis, included: Golf (21), Fishing (10), Karate (10), Sailing (10), Trampoline (10), Hockey (9), Netball (8), Cricket (7), Shooting (7), Skiing (7), Basketball (6), Cross country running (6), Ice skating (6), Archery (5), Kick boxing (5), Rugby (4), Canoeing (3), Squash (3), BMX [stunt bike] riding (4) Bowling (2), Diving (2), Fox hunting (2), Judo (2), Water polo (2), Wrestling (2), Baseball (1), Kayaking (1), Lacrosse (1) and Rock climbing (1).
- *Cars and motorbikes* included: War hammer (20), Mechanical things (3) and Go carting (2).
- *Youth organisations* included those who were Air Cadets or who were members of the Brigades, Brownies, Cadets, Guides and Scouts.

- *Outside hobbies* included: Walking (9), Farming (7), Gardening (3), Climbing trees/walls (2), Building site working (1), Camping (1), Duke of Edinburgh (1) and Kite flying (1).
- *Skate/snow boarding* included: Roller blading (4).
- *Animals* included: taking dogs for a walk (2 people), bird watching (1) and budgie breeding (1).

Table A4/8: Age young people allowed unsupervised activity (Page 86)
(See Figure 5.5)

	(1)	(2)	(3)	(4)	(5)	(6)
5 to 9 years	32	9	4	3	1	0
10 or 11 years	36	17	17	10	3	1
12 or 13 years	22	29	35	26	9	3
14 or 15 years	7	30	33	40	34	10
16 or over	2	14	10	18	39	47
NEVER allowed	1	1	1	3	14	39
Average age	10.4	12.8	13.0	13.6	15.8	16.3

(1) = Allowed to go to alone without an adult or much older child

(2) = Allowed to go out alone in the evening to a friend's/anywhere

(3) = Allowed to go to town centre without an adult or much older child

(4) = Allowed to stay at home in the evening without adult to supervise

(5) = Allowed to stay at home overnight without adult to supervise

(6) = Allowed to stay out overnight without parents' knowing whereabouts

Table A4/9: Age when Tweenagers first had sex (Page 89)

Age at time of survey	11 or under	12	13	14	15	Total who had had sex	Base
13	10	18	25	–	–	53	585
14	29	27	70	60	–	186	1,035
15	12	13	26	44	22	117	450
Total	51	58	121	104	22	356	2,070
Percentage	15	16	34	29	6	100%	

Table A4/10: Percentage attending week night activities in a church hall
by church attendance (Page 94)   (Questions 19 and 30a)

	Regular %	Occasional %	Lapsed %	Never %	Overall %
Sunday School	49	11	4	1	20
Youth Club	30	19	16	10	19
Youth Group	39	12	13	7	19
Out of School Club	15	17	18	12	14
Scouts or Guides	21	17	9	4	13
Drama/music groups	18	12	15	5	12
Holiday clubs	15	11	7	5	9
Camp. Crus. Path.	12	4	3	1	6
Boys/ Girls' Brigade	8	7	4	3	5
Rock Solid Clubs	7	5	4	3	4

Camp. Crus. Path. = Campaigners, Crusaders and Pathfinders

Table A4/11: Percentage attending week night activities in a church hall by age (Page 94)
(Questions 1 and 30a)

	10 %	11 %	12 %	13 %	14 %	Overall %
Sunday School	35	25	18	16	14	20
Youth Club	14	20	25	22	23	19
Youth Group	11	20	25	22	28	19
Out of School Club	17	17	18	11	13	14
Scouts or Guides	20	19	10	10	9	13
Drama/music groups	16	15	12	10	15	12
Holiday clubs	20	11	11	5	7	9
Camp. Crus. Path.	7	6	6	5	6	6
Boys'/Girls' Brigade	11	4	6	3	4	5
Rock Solid Clubs	3	4	7	4	4	4

Table A4/12: Percentage regularly attending week night activities in a church hall by Christian belief (Page 96)   (Questions 30a and 31)

	Regular attender?	God %	Heaven %	Jesus %	Reincarnation %
Sunday School	YES	95	90	93	13
	NO	67	69	61	32
Youth Club	YES	73	81	79	28
	NO		72	65	
Youth Group	YES	89	86	89	19
	NO	69	70	62	30
Out of School Club	YES	73	74	68	28
	NO				
Scouts or Guides	YES	73	74	83	28
	NO			65	
Drama/music groups	YES	84	86	79	28
	NO	71	72	66	
Holiday clubs	YES	90	85	68	28
	NO	71	72		
Camp. Crus. Path.	YES	94	89	92	12
	NO	72	73	66	29
Boys'/Girls' Brigade	YES	85	74	88	28
	NO	71		67	
Rock Solid Clubs	YES	73	74	68	28
	NO				
Overall		73	74	68	28

Where figures did not vary by regularity of church attendance, the percentage is put in the middle of the row.

Table A4/13: Years attending church before leaving (Page 111)
(Questions 20a and 24)

Start age	<1	2	3	4	5	6	7	8	9	10	11	12	13	14	Avge
				Numbers of years in church before leaving											
0	0	2	2	1	2	2	2	2	9	6	8	4	7	4	9.6
1	2	2	1	1	5	4	6	9	12	4	1	1	1	–	7.3
2	1	0	2	4	2	5	3	4	2	2	0	1	–	–	6.3
3	5	3	5	9	5	6	4	2	2	1	0	–	–	–	4.6
4	6	14	8	6	6	3	4	6	0	0	–	–	–	–	3.9
5	0	3	0	3	1	9	4	4	0	–	–	–	–	–	5.7
6	6	7	7	6	1	2	1	0	–	–	–	–	–	–	3.0
7	6	5	4	3	1	2	0	–	–	–	–	–	–	–	2.7
8	9	1	2	0	1	0	–	–	–	–	–	–	–	–	1.7
9	9	2	2	1	1	–	–	–	–	–	–	–	–	–	1.9
10	8	0	3	0	–	–	–	–	–	–	–	–	–	–	1.5
11	5	1	0	–	–	–	–	–	–	–	–	–	–	–	1.2
12	4	2	–	–	–	–	–	–	–	–	–	–	–	–	1.3
13	0	–	–	–	–	–	–	–	–	–	–	–	–	–	–
Total	61	42	36	34	25	33	24	27	25	13	9	6	8	4	5.1

Table A4/14: Age by denomination of church attended (Page 120)
(Questions 1 and 25)

	10 years %	11 years %	12 years %	13 years %	14 years %
Church of England	17	21	21	23	18
Roman Catholic	16	13	31	26	14
Baptist	21	19	26	20	14
Pentecostal	13	19	23	36	9
Independent	16	8	20	20	36
New Church	35	27	15	12	11
Methodist	14	27	14	31	14

Table A4/15: Reasons for church attendance by age (Page 118)
(Questions 1 and 27)

Reason	10 %	11 %	12 %	13 %	14 %	Overall %
They have always gone	60	72	73	75	78	72
To learn about God	76	71	67	62	61	67
Their parents send them	33	56	61	63	64	56
To sing hymns	28	33	25	23	20	26

Table A4/16: Church activities by usual Grade achieved (Page 125)
(Questions 3 and 28)

Activity	Grade			Average times a year		
	A %	B %	C–F %	A	B	C–F
Pray to God	17	30	43	201	150	144
Read part of the Bible	25	45	57	86	55	58
Attend a church-based youth group	40	54	58	61	48	44
Take an active part in church services	37	56	63	27	26	34
Lead a church-based youth group	86	92	89	46	44	64

Table A4/17: Church activities by Christian commitment (Page 125)
(Questions 17 and 28)

	Commitment					Average times a year				
Activity	Certain %	Unsure %	Lapsed %	Not Christian %	Other religion %	Certain	Unsure	Lapsed	Not Christian	Other religion
Pray to God	11	32	64	68	25	197	115	77	83	184
Read part of the Bible[2]	23	44	76	77	60	75	46	86[1]	36	117
Attend a church-based youth group	32	54	91	83	75	56	44	n/a	51	67
Take active part in church services	32	58	89	84	72	28	19	n/a	32	33
Attend a Bible Study Group	74	85	94	95	82	48	57	n/a	n/a	72
Lead a church-based youth group	86	91	96	96	96	44	54	n/a	n/a	n/a

Not Christian = I am not a Christian   Other religion = I belong to another religion
[1] *Based on very small numbers, and therefore not reliable*
[2] *Or other Holy Book when belonging to another religion*

Table A4/18: Church activities by age (Page 125)
(Questions 1 and 28)

	Age					Average times a year				
Activity	10 %	11 %	12 %	13 %	14 %	10	11	12	13	14
Pray to God	11	25	28	35	30	199	167	162	171	143
Take active part in church services	40	45	51	53	55	35	28	28	21	21

Table A4/19:
Assessment of friends' reaction to churchgoing by Christian commitment (Page 127)
(Questions 17 and 30b)

	Certain %	Unsure %	Lapsed %	Never %	Overall %
I have already told my friends that I go to church	47	22	10	7	33
They might make fun of me or think I am stupid or uncool	26	38	52	43	32
They might be curious and ask me questions	14	17	14	24	16
I would be too shy to tell anyone	4	9	4	8	6
They belong to another religion so they would not be bothered	2	3	2	4	3
Other ways	7	11	18	14	10

Table A4/20: Assessment of friends' reaction to churchgoing by age (Page 128)
(Questions 1 and 30b)

	10 %	11 %	12 %	13 %	14 %	Overall %
I have already told my friends that I go to church	45	31	31	30	35	33
They might make fun of me or think I am stupid or uncool	25	30	30	39	35	32
They might be curious and ask me questions	16	16	16	16	18	16
I would be too shy to tell anyone	8	8	4	5	8	6
They belong to another religion so they would not be bothered	5	3	3	2	2	3
Other ways	1	12	16	8	2	10

Table A4/21: What their friends would say about their going to church
by how Tweenagers described their home (Page 128)   (Questions 14 and 30b)

	(1) %	(2) %	(3) %	(4) %	(5) %	Overall %
I have already told my friends that I go to church	37	27	36	22	14	33
They might make fun of me or think I am stupid or uncool	28	37	30	42	54	32
They might be curious and ask me questions	17	17	15	18	12	16
I would be too shy to tell anyone	6	6	6	5	4	6
They belong to another religion so they would not be bothered	2	4	4	5	5	3
Other ways	10	9	9	8	11	10

(1) = I feel secure and loved
(2) = Sometimes I feel loved
(3) = Trying to love each other
(4) = Would rather be elsewhere
(5) = Comfortable, but not close

*Table A4/22: Personal attitudes and actions by age: percentage who **agree** (Page 141)*
(Questions 1 and 9)

	10 %	11 %	12 %	13 %	14 %	Overall %
Stealing is always wrong	84	79	73	67	64	73
It is always wrong to cheat	79	74	63	62	62	67
Sometimes you have to tell a lie	55	61	71	73	72	66
Life's too short to worry	33	36	43	49	56	43
It is always wrong to tell lies	64	49	40	32	27	42
It is OK to copy things from other people if you are in a hurry	11	18	30	29	35	24
It is OK to take little things like pencils from school	8	7	13	12	20	12

Table A4/23:

*Personal attitudes and actions by church attendance: percentage who **agree** (Page 141)*
(Questions 19 and 9)

	(1) %	(2) %	(3) %	(4) %	*Overall* %
Stealing is always wrong	80	70	71	68	73
It is always wrong to cheat	75	65	67	60	67
Sometimes you have to tell a lie	56	70	77	72	66
The main purpose in life is enjoyment and personal fulfilment	44	56	63	62	55
Life's too short to worry	34	44	50	51	43
It is always wrong to tell lies	51	43	36	35	42
In times of trouble or crisis I feel alone	32	39	45	35	36
It is OK to copy things from other people if you are in a hurry	17	23	30	33	24
One person cannot really make a difference in this world	17	23	24	28	22
It is OK to take little things like pencils from school	7	11	15	16	12

(1) = Regular attender   (2) = Occasional   (3) = Lapsed   (4) = Never

Table A4/24:

*Personal attitudes and actions by denomination: percentage who **agree** (Page 142)*
(Questions 19 and 25)

	(1) %	(2) %	(3) %	(4) %	(5) %	*Overall* %
Sometimes you have to tell a lie	67	78	47	73	54	66
The main purpose in life is enjoyment & personal fulfilment	54	63	33	60	56	55

(1) = Church of England   (2) = Catholic   (3) = Baptist   (4) = Methodist   (5) = Others

Table A4/25:
*Personal attitudes and actions by usual grades: percentage who **agree** (Page 142)*
(Questions 3 and 9)

Statement	As %	Bs %	Cs %	D–Fs %	Overall %
Stealing is always wrong	78	71	63	62	73
The main purpose in life is enjoyment and personal fulfilment	50	58	58	47	55
It is better to get even than mad	33	39	47	42	38
My opinions and attitudes are not taken seriously	25	26	34	33	27
The future will be better than today	21	27	35	30	25
It is OK to copy things from other people if you are in a hurry	21	25	32	44	24
One person cannot really make a difference in this world	18	22	30	42	22
It is OK to take little things like pencils from school	10	11	19	16	12

Table A4/26: Helping other people by church attendance (Page 143)
(Questions 10 and 17)

Helping other people around where I live	Regular %	Occasional %	Lapsed %	Never %	Overall %
YES, through my school	41	32	31	24	33
YES, through church	42	13	5	2	19
YES, through other groups	28	21	12	8	18
NO	26	37	45	54	38

[1] *Helping others "on my own" did not vary by church attendance*

Table A4/27:
Actions on finding money by gender and grades usually obtained (Page 145)
(Questions 2 and 3 and 11)

	Finding one £20 note				Finding two £50 notes			
	Leave it there	Give it to charity	Keep it	Hand in to police	Leave it there	Give it to charity	Keep it	Hand in to police
Gender/Grade	%	%	%	%	%	%	%	%
Male	4	10	67	19	9	7	50	34
Female	5	16	51	28	10	9	32	49
Overall	**5**	**13**	**58**	**24**	**10**	**8**	**40**	**42**
Mostly As	7	15	51	27	11	9	32	48
Mostly Bs	4	12	62	22	10	8	41	41
Mostly C–Fs	2	9	72	17	6	5	61	28

Table A4/28: Actions on finding money by church attendance (Page 145)
(Questions 11 and 17)

	Finding one £20 note				Finding two £50 notes			
	Leave it there	Give it to charity	Keep it	Hand in to police	Leave it there	Give it to charity	Keep it	Hand in to police
Churchgoing	%	%	%	%	%	%	%	%
Regular	8	17	40	35	9	9	24	58
Occasional	4	13	59	24	11	8	39	42
Lapsed	4	11	66	19	9	8	46	37
Never	2	9	77	12	10	7	60	23
Overall	**5**	**13**	**58**	**24**	**10**	**8**	**40**	**42**

Table A4/29:
What Tweenagers would do with money they found by internet use (Page 145)
(Questions 7 and 11)

	Finding one £20 note				Finding two £50 notes			
Internet use	Leave it there %	Give it to charity %	Keep it %	Hand in to police %	Leave it there %	Give it to charity %	Keep it %	Hand in to police %
More than once a day	5	8	71	16	4	9	60	27
Once a day	5	12	64	19	11	9	43	37
Once a week	6	13	56	25	10	8	37	45
Once a month or less	4	17	50	29	10	7	32	51
Overall	5	13	58	24	10	8	40	42

Table A4/30: Incorrect activities by age (Page 148)
(Questions 1 and 16)

	10 %	11 %	12 %	13 %	14 %	Overall %
Watch horror films	59	64	72	78	77	69
Lie to adults	41	50	63	65	67	56
Drink to get drunk	4	6	20	28	45	20
Cheat in exam/ test	7	10	18	20	22	15
Smoked a cigarette	2	6	13	20	24	13
Used an illegal drug	0	2	7	7	15	6

Table A4/31: Incorrect activities by usual grades (Page 149) – (Questions 3 and 16)

	Mostly As %	Mostly Bs %	Mostly C–Fs %	Overall %
Watch horror films	65	73	83	69
Drink to get drunk	15	22	34	20
Smoked a cigarette	8	13	29	13
Stolen money	5	7	17	7
Used an illegal drug	4	5	15	6
Been shoplifting	3	5	13	5

Table A4/32: Incorrect activities by church attendance (Page 150)
(Questions 16 and 19)

	Regular %	Occasional %	Lapsed %	Never %	Overall %
Watch horror films	51	76	80	85	69
Drink to get drunk	8	20	28	31	20
Hurt someone physically	14	15	18	25	17
Smoked a cigarette	6	12	18	20	13
Stolen money	3	7	10	12	7
Used an illegal drug	1	4	8	11	6
Been shoplifting	2	5	6	8	5

Table A4/33: Belief by Christian commitment (Page 160)
(Questions 17 and 31a)

I believe in...	Certain %	Unsure %	Lapsed %	Never %	Other faith %	Overall %
Heaven	85	70	39	42	56	73
God	88	66	25	31	76	72
Jesus	85	61	22	28	24	67
Hell	56	47	39	39	40	50
The Devil	49	39	35	38	28	43
Reincarnation	24	31	47	35	37	28

Table A4/34: Belief by grades usually obtained (Page 161, Note 5)
(Questions 3 and 31a)

	Mostly As %	Mostly Bs %	Mostly C–Fs %	Overall %
Heaven	78	70	68	73
God	80	68	58	72
Jesus	73	63	56	67

Table A4/35: Belief by churchgoing (Page 162, Note 7)
(Questions 19 and 31a)

I believe in...	Regular %	Occasional %	Lapsed %	Never %	Overall %
Heaven	91	70	69	51	73
God	95	76	65	42	72
Jesus	92	69	56	36	67
Hell	59	48	47	42	50
The Devil	53	34	41	37	43
Reincarnation	15	33	35	40	28

Table A4/36: How God is pictured by age (Page 166)
(Questions 1 and 32)

	1992 RAKT			2001 RAKES					Overall	
	12 %	13 %	14 %	10 %	11 %	12 %	13 %	14 %	1992[1] %	2001 %
Father	56	55	58	69	64	55	57	65	56	61
Friend	n/a	n/a	n/a	66	60	53	50	54	n/a	56
Base	277	263	125	361	414	484	459	320	665	2,038

[1] *Based on the years 12 to 14 only*

Table A4/37: How God is pictured by school grades and description of home (Page 167)
(Questions 3, 15 and 32)

Usual grade/My home is where...	Creator	Father	Friend	Love	Saviour	Judge	Base
Mostly As	75	70	64	58	47	31	623
Mostly Bs	62	56	50	46	33	23	929
Mostly C–Fs	54	54	50	44	28	15	257
I feel secure and loved	69	65	60				1,196
Sometimes I feel loved	61	56	52		No		470
Trying to love each other	68	61	55		significant		174
Would rather be elsewhere	45	48	45		variations		84
Comfortable, but not close	51	51	39				85
Overall	62	61	56	48	35	22	1,809

Table A4/38: What makes someone a Christian by churchgoing (Page 171)
(Questions 19 and 34)

What makes a person a Christian?	Regular %	Occasional %	Lapsed %	Never %	Overall %
Believing in God	81	69	68	57	70
Being baptised/christened	46	58	56	57	53
Believing the Bible is true	62	48	49	43	52
Knowing Jesus as a personal saviour	63	35	37	31	45
Being born in a Christian family	20	34	35	36	29
Going to a Christian school	8	17	20	18	15
Being born in the UK	1	3	5	6	3
Don't know	3	6	8	15	7

"Going to church", "Leading a good life", "Saying that they are Christian" and "Something else" did not vary by churchgoing frequency.

Table A4/39: Religious experience by churchgoing (Page 173)
(Questions 19 and 36a)

What makes a person a Christian?	Regular %	Occasional %	Lapsed %	Never %	Overall %
A feeling of peace during a service	61	39	26	7	38
Experience of becoming a Christian	52	33	28	12	35
The presence of God	54	25	19	12	32
Feeling as if somebody/something was trying to communicate with you	35	29	36	22	31
An experience to do with nature	23	27	24	16	22
Other spiritual/supernatural force	17	22	25	20	20
A healing experience	20	17	12	8	15

"Visions/voices/strange dreams", "Something beyond description" and "Something else" did not vary by churchgoing frequency.

Table A4/40: Confirmands by age band and environment[1] (Page 164, Note 17)

Environment	Under 14 %	14–17 %	Adult %
Rural	50	26	24
Suburban	40	19	41
Urban	35	19	46

[1]From article "The Rural Church is different: the case of Anglican Confirmation" by Leslie Francis and David Lankshear, *Journal of Empirical Theology*, Volume 10, Number 1, 1997, Table 1.

Table A4/41: Self-image by age (Page 184, Note 2) (Questions 1 and 12a)

Trait	10 %	11 %	12 %	13 %	14 %	Overall %
Sporty	60	58	53	50	42	52
Playful	63	54	49	44	40	49
Mature	37	43	46	52	52	45
Lazy	33	28	40	43	37	36
Unusual	23	19	30	29	28	26
Leader	14	21	27	26	30	23
Unforgiving	5	6	10	6	8	7
Total number (=100%)	361	414	484	459	320	2,038

Table A4/42: Self-image by gender (Page 184, Note 3)
(Questions 2 and 12a)

Trait	M %	F %	All %	Trait	M %	F %	All %
Friendly	77	90	82	Sporty	62	45	52
Caring	50	76	63	Well-behaved	42	53	48
Helpful	52	63	57	Mature	41	50	45
Reliable	52	63	57	Moody	19	36	28
Talkative	46	68	57	Bossy	12	28	20
Hard-working	51	61	56	Fussy	13	26	20
Thoughtful	47	61	54	Scared	8	14	11

M = Male F = Female

Table A4/43: Self-image by religious commitment (Page 185, Note 5)
(Questions 12a and 17)

Trait	Christian %	Unsure %	Lapsed %	Never %	Other faith %	All %
Caring	69	60	48	51	65	63
Helpful	62	53	52	50	62	57
Hard-working	61	53	34	50	58	56
Well-behaved	52	46	28	41	46	48
Rude	11	15	17	22	20	14
Unforgiving	4	9	19	11	9	7
Bully	2	2	4	7	10	3

Table A4/44: Self-image by church attendance (Page 186, Note 6)
(Questions 12a and 19)

Trait	Regular %	Occasional %	Lapsed %	Never %	All %
Caring	70	57	67	56	63
Well-behaved	56	46	42	44	48
Daring	30	38	39	41	36
Lazy	30	38	41	41	36
Rude	8	16	16	21	14
Perfect	7	10	11	16	10
Unforgiving	3	6	10	11	7

Table A4/45: Self-image by grades usually achieved (Page 185, Note 4)
(Questions 3 and 12a)

Trait	As %	Bs %	C–Fs %	All %	Trait	As %	Bs %	C–Fs %	All %
Friendly	86	84	73	82	Lazy	28	39	51	36
Caring	72	62	53	63	Leader	31	22	19	23
Helpful	66	55	49	57	Peaceful	21	12	13	15
Reliable	69	56	44	57	Angry	11	13	24	14
Hard-working	76	51	35	56	Rude	10	15	23	14
Thoughtful	64	53	41	54	Slow	7	8	16	9
Well-behaved	61	43	34	48	Unforgiving	6	6	14	7
Mature	61	43	31	45	Bully	2	3	9	3
Noisy	37	47	52	43					

About Christian Research

Christian Research began in 1993, but continued the aims of its predecessor MARC Europe which began ten years earlier in April 1983. Christian Research is an independent registered charity (Number 101 7701) and a company limited by guarantee (Number 279 2246). It is committed to:

- Collecting data about church and Christian agencies
- Interpreting the results and suggesting actions so that the Kingdom of God may grow
- Publishing resource volumes every two years like *Religious Trends* and the *UK Christian Handbook* (www.ukchristian-handbook.org.uk)

We serve all sections of the church in the Trinitarian group – Anglicans, Roman Catholics, Orthodox, Methodists, Baptists, United Reformed, and many smaller denominations. We do not do research for non-Trinitarian churches such as the Jehovah's Witnesses or Mormons.

We are particularly well known for our large scale surveys of Church Attendance in the various countries of the United Kingdom, the most recent of which have been the English Church Attendance Survey of 1998 (whose results were published in *The Tide is Running Out*) and the Scottish Church Census of 2002. Full details of our work may be seen on our website www.christian-research.org.uk.

Recent publications include:

- *The Tide is Running Out,* Christian Research, London, January 2000
- *Steps to the Future,* March 2000, co-published with Scripture Union, Milton Keynes

- *Twelve Things about Society which impact the Church,* February 2001
- *Twelve Ideas to help 'turn the tide',* March 2001
- *Eve's Glue,* Heather Wraight, October 2001, co-published with Paternoster Lifestyle, Carlisle
- *UK Christian Handbook* 2002/2003 edition, edited by Heather Wraight, November 2001
- *Religious Trends* No 3, 2002/2003 edition, edited by Peter Brierley, November 2001
- *101 statistics that every church leader should know,* April 2002
- *Training Leaders to Think Strategically,* Major-General Richard Dannant, April 2002
- *Building Vision: How to think Strategically,* forthcoming

Christian Research has a Board of 11 people. Its current chair is the Rt Rev John Flack, Bishop of Huntingdon. Christian Research has a staff of five people, and was started, and is currently headed by Dr Peter Brierley, its Executive Director, a statistician with 35 years' experience working on Christian evaluation, research and publishing. Heather Wraight, who worked in communication for over 20 years, joined him in 1994 and is now Deputy Director.

For more information either visit our website as given above, write to us at Vision Building, 4 Footscray Road, Eltham, London SE9 2TZ, phone us on 020 8294 1989, fax us on 020 8294 0014, or email us: admin@christian-research.org.uk

Index

If a number has "n" or "ns" after it this refers to the footnote or footnotes on that page. Thus "180n3" means Footnote 3 on Page 180.